At Issue

Piracy on the High Seas

Other Books in the At Issue Series:

At Issue

Piracy on the High Seas

Debra A. Miller, Book Editor

GREENHAVEN PRESS
A part of Gale, Cengage Learning

GALE
CENGAGE Learning·

Farmington Hills, Mich • San Francisco • New York • Waterville, Maine
Meriden, Conn • Mason, Ohio • Chicago

Elizabeth Des Chenes, *Director, Content Strategy*
Douglas Dentino, *Manager, New Product*

© 2014 Greenhaven Press, a part of Gale, Cengage Learning.

WCN: 01-100-101

Gale and Greenhaven Press are registered trademarks used herein under license.

For more information, contact:
Greenhaven Press
27500 Drake Rd.
Farmington Hills, MI 48331-3535
Or you can visit our Internet site at gale.cengage.com

For product information and technology assistance, contact us at

Gale Customer Support, 1-800-877-4253
For permission to use material from this text or product, submit all requests online at www.cengage.com/permissions.

Further permissions questions can be e-mailed to permissionrequest@cengage.com.

Articles in Greenhaven Press anthologies are often edited for length to meet page requirements. In addition, original titles of these works are changed to clearly present the main thesis and to explicitly indicate the author's opinion. Every effort is made to ensure that Greenhaven Press accurately reflects the original intent of the authors. Every effort has been made to trace the owners of copyrighted material.

Cover photograph copyright © Images.com/Corbis.

LIBRARY OF CONGRESS CATALOGING-IN-PUBLICATION DATA

Piracy on the high seas / Debra A. Miller, Book Editor.
      pages cm. -- (At issue)
   Includes bibliographical references and index.
   ISBN 978-0-7377-6848-0 (hardcover) -- ISBN 978-0-7377-6849-7 (pbk.)
  1. Maritime terrorism. 2. Piracy. 3. Hijacking of ships. I. Miller, Debra A.
   HV6433.785.P572 2014
   364.16'4--dc23
                                                          2013044018

Printed in the United States of America
1 2 3 4 5 6 7 18 17 16 15 14

Contents

Introduction

Piracy generally refers to robbery, kidnapping, or violence conducted at sea or against coastal towns. The crime of piracy has existed throughout history, ever since human civilizations first took to the seas for trade and conquest. For more than a century during the 1600s and 1700s, however, thousands of pirates operated in the Caribbean and Mediterranean Seas—a period often called the Golden Age of piracy. Piracy declined significantly thereafter, but a new wave of modern piracy has emerged in recent decades, in the waters off the coast of the North African nation of Somalia, and most recently in the ocean near West Africa.

The world's first pirates attacked trading routes of the ancient Greeks and Romans, seizing grain, olive oil, and other goods. Later during the Middle Ages, the Vikings became famous for sea-based aggression against both ships and coastal communities. Beginning in the seveneeth century, during the so-called Golden Age, piracy truly reached its apex. At that time, piracy became a commonplace activity as government-sanctioned pirates attacked ships on the high seas and in coastal areas. Some of the first pirates of this era were Frenchmen called buccaneers who settled on the Caribbean island of Hispaniola, today the countries of Haiti and the Dominican Republic. The buccaneers initially survived by hunting but later turned to pirate attacks in the Caribbean Sea on Spanish ships filled with New World treasure. Later, buccaneers were authorized by English governors of the Caribbean island of Jamaica to continue the plunder of Spanish treasure ships.

Other pirates during this period were privateers—European seamen with private gunships who were issued commissions, called letters of marque, by European governments, giving them permission to attack and rob ships of specific enemy nations. The profits would then be shared between the privateer and the government. One of the most famous privateers was Sir Francis Drake—a British sea captain who was commissioned by Great Britain's Queen Elizabeth I to raid Spanish ships and possessions. Viewed as a hero in Britain but hated by Spain for his acts of piracy, Drake went down in history as the first Englishman to circumnavigate the globe when he sailed to South America in 1577 and then returned to England by crossing the Pacific Ocean. Privateers like Drake flourished between the sixteenth and eighteenth centuries when European countries were almost constantly at war with each other. Later, however, after peace was established in Europe, many privateers fell on hard times. When their government commissions ended, they continued their careers as pirates robbing and kidnapping for solely private gain.

Perhaps the most famous pirates during this Golden Age were the Barbary pirates, also called "corsairs," who terrorized Christian ships in the Mediterranean Sea. The corsairs operated from bases in the North African states of Tripoli, Tunis, Morocco, and Algiers—the area known as the Barbary Coast—routinely attacking European and American merchant ships, stealing their cargo, and kidnapping crewmembers as slaves. Most of the Barbary corsairs were Berbers, Arabs, and Muslims from North Africa, but some were actually former European privateers. The corsairs found convenient bases along the Barbary Coast to shelter their ships and sell their pirate booty, and they were given sanctuary by the various North African states as long as they shared their stolen treasure and slaves with those rulers.

Beginning in 1662, European countries negotiated a series of treaties that protected them from Barbary piracy if they paid a ransom or bribe, called a tribute, to the Barbary states. For many decades, European countries paid these tributes rather than risk attacks, and after the American Revolution, the new United States, under President George Washington and President John Adams, also paid tributes to the Barbary states to protect American ships. The United States finally broke free of the Barbary pirate tribute system under the leadership of President Thomas Jefferson. Jefferson refused to pay any more tributes, instead deciding to build up a US naval force. Using this new navy, the United States declared war against Tripoli and Algiers, leading to an 1806 treaty with Tripoli that contained the problem of piracy for the next decade. Barbary piracy was not fully vanquished, however, until the United States won a second Barbary war in 1815, leading to treaties ending US tributes to all the Barbary states.

Following the Barbary period, piracy was no longer a major problem for shipping nations during most of the nineteenth and twentieth centuries. In the late 1990s, however, a modern version of piracy erupted, with the number of pirate attacks increasing each year. Most of these pirate attacks occurred in the waters off the coast of Somalia, a poverty-stricken and politically unstable nation in East Africa situated near major trade routes in the Gulf of Aden, a deep body of water that connects the Red Sea with the Indian Ocean. In the ensuing years, Somali pirates became known for increasingly violent attacks on international trade ships passing through this region. These modern pirates have reaped huge profits from taking hostages and demanding high ransoms. In 2010, for example, a total of 445 pirate attacks were reported, during which pirates captured fifty-three ships and took a total of 1,181 hostages. Over the years, the Somali pirate attacks have caused great trauma and numerous deaths to sailors and cost the international community billions of dollars each year—in ransoms paid by shipping companies, in extra shipping expenses for insurance and armed guards, and in the expense of international naval patrols organized to deter pirate attacks.

International and private efforts to stop Somali piracy appear to be working, causing a steep decline in successful attacks in 2012 and 2013, but recently another type of piracy has begun in the Atlantic Ocean off the coast of West Africa.

Here, pirates are focusing on stealing ship cargo, often oil, rather than taking hostages for ransom. Many of the pirates hail from Nigeria, the site of an oil boom, and attack Nigerian oil shipments. As the oil boom has spread to other countries in the region, piracy has spread to the waters of other West African nations.

The issue of modern piracy is the subject of *At Issue: Piracy on the High Seas*. Authors of viewpoints included in this volume address topics such as the cost of piracy, the connection between piracy and terrorism, whether antipiracy efforts have been successful, and how the international community should respond in the future.

1

Somali Pirates Cost Global Economy "$18 Billion a Year"

Teo Kermeliotis

Teo Kermeliotis is a contributing journalist to CNN, an American news organization and website.

Hijackings of commercial ships by Somali pirates near the Horn of Africa have declined since 2011, but according to a report released in April 2013 by the World Bank—"Pirates of Somalia: Ending the Threat, Rebuilding a Nation"—piracy could still cost the global economy as much as $18 billion each year. Piracy makes international shipping more expensive—by causing ships to change their trade routes to avoid pirate areas, adding to fuel costs, and creating higher insurance rates and extra payments for ship security guards. Pirate attacks also have negatively affected area tourism and fishing economies in Somalia and other East African coastal countries. The report finds that the only solution to piracy in this region is to rebuild Somalia's failing political and economic systems.

The Somali pirates roaming the waters off the Horn of Africa push global trade costs up by billions of dollars per year and severely affect the economic activities of neighboring countries, a new World Bank report has found.

Although hijackings in the region have dropped significantly since last year [2011], piracy could still cost the global economy an estimated $18 billion annually, according to the "Pirates of Somalia: Ending the Threat, Rebuilding a Nation" report, launched Thursday [April 11, 2013] in the Somali capital of Mogadishu.

The Economic Cost of Piracy

The increased costs come as shippers are forced to change trading routes, sending fuel bills soaring, as well as pay higher insurance premiums and security bills for guards on board.

But apart from making international trade more expensive, the threat of piracy in one of the world's most important trade gateways is also an economic blow for neighboring East African countries, particularly in the pillar sectors of tourism and fishing, said the report.

Since 2006, tourism spending in East African coastal countries has risen 25% more slowly than other sub-Saharan African nations, mainly because of fewer arrivals from high-income citizens of OECD [Organization for Economic Cooperation and Development] countries. Piracy in the region is thought to have tarnished its image as a stable holiday destination, with visits to impacted East African coastal nations down by nearly 6.5% relative to visits to other countries.

The solution to ending piracy will only come with the recreation of a functional Somali state.

According to the World Bank, exports of fish products from piracy-hit countries have also suffered, declining by 23.8% since 2006, the year the report takes as the starting point of piracy.

The World Bank defines piracy-affected countries as Comoros, Djibouti, Kenya, Mozambique, Madagascar, Mauritius, the Seychelles, Somalia, Tanzania, as well as Yemen, Pakistan and the countries of the Persian Gulf.

The economy of war-torn Somalia, which last September [2012] moved closer to stability after electing its first president on home soil in decades, is also severely hit; piracy-related trade costs increase by up to $6 million annually, without considering that potential sea-based economic activities are constrained by piracy.

Help Needed for Somalia

The authors of the report said the solution to ending piracy will only come with the recreation of a functional Somali state and urged the international community to focus on helping the East African country build a viable political system.

"Piracy is a symptom of the breakdown of Somalia's political system," said economist and lead author of the report Quy-Toan Do. "Go after the system, not just the pirates."

According to the report, 1,068 attacks have been carried out by Somali pirates since January 2005. Of these, 218 resulted in successful hijackings, with an estimated $53 million average annual ransom paid. Between 82 and 97 casualties are believed to have occurred as a result of these attacks.

Attacks peaked in 2011, but have declined sharply since, largely because of increased mobilization of international naval forces and tighter security adopted by the shipping industry.

A report earlier this week by advocacy group Oceans Beyond Piracy said that maritime piracy cost the global economy between $5.7 and $6.1 billion in 2012, much lower than the World Bank figures.

2

Piracy Takes a Heavy Human Toll

Kaija Hurlburt and D. Conor Seyle

Kaija Hurlburt is the project manager for the Oceans Beyond Piracy (OBP) project at the One Earth Future (OEF) Foundation, a think tank founded in 2007 to advocate for more effective systems of governance to achieve a world beyond war. D. Conor Seyle is an associate director of research and development at OEF.

Pirate attacks off the coast of Somalia declined dramatically in 2012, but piracy continues to pose difficult challenges for seafarers, fishermen, and their families. In 2012 and 2013, fifty-seven hostages were released, some of whom had been held captive for multiple years. After these releases, however, Somali pirates continued to hold at least seventy-eight hostages. Meanwhile, seafarers traveling through pirate areas off the coast of Somalia and in the Gulf of Guinea still face the threat of attacks from pirates, which can result in physical harm, death, or being taken hostage for ransom. Often, for these unfortunate individuals and their families, the initial attack is only the start of a long road of hardship. If a ship's crewmember is taken hostage, the victim usually must endure daily physical and psychological abuse— including physical beatings and periodic threats of execution. In addition, their families typically face both prolonged emotional trauma and financial problems due to loss of income from their loved one who is held hostage.

Piracy off the coast of Somalia saw a dramatic decline in the number of attacks in 2012. This translates to improved circumstances for seafarers transiting these waters. This report ["The Human Cost of Maritime Piracy 2012"] seeks to recognize this positive trend, while highlighting the ongoing challenges that seafarers, fishermen, and their families continue to face because of piracy. It builds on previous versions of the report by including a new section on the impact to seafarers and fishermen in the Gulf of Guinea region.

Fifty-seven hostages were released in 2012 and 2013, all of whom had been flagged in the 2011 report on the Human Cost of Somali Piracy because they faced an especially high risk of abuse or trauma. It is important to celebrate the long-awaited release of these hostages. These included the surviving 22 seafarers aboard *MV Iceberg I*, who experienced the deaths of two crewmates and who endured 1,000 days in captivity. Additionally, the six crewmembers from the *MV Leopard* were released after 839 days in captivity, during which time they had been forced to participate in videos about their fears and hardships, knowing that the videos would be watched by their loved ones back home, thereby causing additional worry and concern. The four crewmembers held back after the release of the *MT Gemini* also gained their freedom after 581 days in captivity, roughly a year of which took place after the release of their other crewmates.

Despite these releases, at least 78 hostages continue to be held captive by Somali pirates and hundreds more continue to face the stress and risk of physical harm associated with being attacked by pirates. There were at least 851 seafarers attacked off the coast of Somalia and 966 seafarers attacked in the Gulf of Guinea region in 2012.

Seafarers and their families suffer many hardships because of piracy. In some cases, the initial attack is just the beginning of the ordeal, especially for those who are taken and held hostage. But this hardship is not limited to the abuse inflicted by the pirates. It can also include financial difficulties during and after the period of captivity, or following a pirate attack, because of disruptions to or cessation of the payment of wages or the loss of personal items. It also includes the psychological trauma, or fear of transiting through pirated waters. This report analyzes these risks based on interviews with and surveys of seafarers. With this information, we hope to draw out the gaps and vulnerable areas that can then be filled by increased support systems for seafarers and their families. . . .

While the number of seafarers attacked and taken hostage dropped 37% in 2012 (after falling 50% the previous year), the rate at which seafarers were ultimately taken hostage after the vessel was fired upon increased from 14% in 2011 to 41% in 2012.

Somali Piracy Attacks

May 10, 2013 marked one full year since a commercial vessel had been hijacked and held for ransom by Somali pirates. While the threat of piracy attacks remains very real, the attack rates overall dropped precipitously in 2012. . . . The number of seafarers involved in reported attacks by pirates off the coast of Somalia decreased by nearly 80% between 2011 and 2012. These figures indicate that there are fewer pirate action groups (PAGs) engaged in piracy. A number of initiatives have been credited for this dramatic drop, including the intelligence-centric and proactive targeting of PAGs by international navies, the increased use of the procedures outlined in the most recent version of the shipping industry's Best Management Practices for Protection against Somalia Based Piracy (BMP), and the increased use of armed security aboard ships. Other factors may include better organized shore-based policing and advances by the new Somali Federal Government and its supporters, which are driving pirates out of their traditional operating areas. . . .

While the number of seafarers attacked and taken hostage dropped 37% in 2012 (after falling 50% the previous year), the rate at which seafarers were ultimately taken hostage after the vessel was fired upon increased from 14% in 2011 to 41% in 2012. In effect, this figure indicates that the success rate of pirate attacks improved at the same time that the total number of attacks where the vessel was fired upon dropped. There are a variety of potential explanations for this shift, including the possibility that the percentage of attacks reported . . . may have decreased. These statistics may also indicate that pirates have learned to fire upon and attack only the more vulnerable vessels, for example vessels that do not carry armed guards or show no evidence of implementing protective measures as per BMP. . . .

Hostages Held Captive in 2012

In 2012 there were 589 people held captive by Somali pirates. This number included the 345 seafarers and fishermen, one journalist, and three aid workers who were captured in 2012. The majority of these hostages were released by mid-2013. Hostages held in 2012 included many who were also included in previous versions of this annual report; this total of 589 included 133 hostages who had been attacked and taken captive in 2010 and 107 hostages who were taken captive in 2011.

As in previous years, the vast majority of people held hostage in 2012 were from developing countries that are not members of the Organization for Economic Cooperation and Development (OECD). . . . However, 2012 saw a substantial decrease in the percentage of hostages from OECD countries; a total of 2%, down from 6% in 2010 and 7% in 2011. . . . For all 589 hostages held in 2012, the average duration of captivity increased to more than 11 months for the 589 hostages held captive by Somali pirates in 2012.

It is promising to see that there have been no vessels taken by Somali pirates in over a year. However, all 78 of the hostages remaining in captivity are classified by OBP [Oceans Beyond Piracy] as High Risk Hostages [held for more than 1 year, held on land, no negotiations for release, or no insurance coverage for a ransom].

This represents an increase from the 60 High Risk Hostages who we reported in 2011. Nearly all (57) of these 2011 High Risk Hostages have fortunately been released, but 75 additional seafarers were classified as High Risk in 2012 due to their prolonged duration of captivity. The remaining 78 High Risk Hostages include 72 seafarers and fishermen, 11 of whom are being held on land without a vessel. There are also six people who were kidnapped by pirate gangs on land rather than taken from vessels, including five aid workers and one journalist, all of whom are believed to also be held on land. All hostages that remain have been in captivity for over a year, and more than half (41 hostages) have been held for over two years.

Captured seafarers suffer violations of their basic human rights to life, liberty and security.

Concern for High Risk Hostages is especially acute because of the extra risks they face due to their extended periods of captivity. These risks include physical impacts from both direct abuse from pirates and health problems resulting from enduring more than a year of limited food, water, and medical support. There is also the psychological challenge of being held by pirates for extended periods of time, which may lead to loss of hope that they will be released.

While the number of attacks may be reduced, the plight for the remaining hostages cannot be forgotten. The goal of counter-piracy operations should be zero hostages; as such, success will not be achieved until all vessels and hostages are released.

Violence Against Hostages

Since there is no consistent system for reporting maritime crime, comprehensive reporting on the extent of violence against hostages is not available. Therefore, in order to provide insight on the specific treatment of hostages, this section looks at reports received from eight ships that were hijacked between 2010 and 2012 and then released from captivity in 2012 or 2013. These reports were submitted to the International Maritime Bureau by [certain countries], ship owners and operators, seafarers, and the Maritime Piracy Humanitarian Response Programme. Due regard has been given to the sensitivities surrounding the identities of the seafarers and their families as well as the vessels, owners, operators, and other parties involved in each hijacking case. Hence the report provides only aggregate information on the treatment of the seafarers and their concerns while in captivity. Statistics regarding these eight ships do not necessarily provide a representative sample of the treatment of all hostages, and therefore this data should be considered illustrative of the kinds of treatment to which seafarers have been exposed. . . .

As in 2011, captured seafarers suffer violations of their basic human rights to life, liberty and security. The seafarers from the eight ships reported upon here were abused both physically and psychologically. The vast majority of the captured crewmembers reported some degree of physical violence ranging from pushing, slapping, and punching to direct assaults that put their lives in danger. They also faced daily psychological abuse. Some seafarers experienced direct threats of execution or other extreme stressors, and even those who did not suffer that degree of abuse faced the uncertainty and stress associated with forced captivity. One seafarer articulated this anxiety by explaining that: "every minute in captivity is a mental pressure." . . .

Physical Abuse

The reports that were received showed significant physical abuse suffered by hostages, especially against those held for longer periods of time. Several seafarers reported physical abuse arising from the pirates' violent reaction to seafarers' inability to meet demands related to ship performance. In one example, a vessel lost both anchors during heavy weather, and the seafarers were beaten and forced to rig the spare anchor using only chain blocks.

In another case, the pirates did not understand the capabilities and limitations of the ship's engine, leading to the continual physical abuse of the engine room crew. The pirates demanded unsustainable speeds resulting in the engine surging, overheating, and finally bursting into flames. Even at this point, it has been reported, the pirates did not allow the crew to stop the engine. They continued to run it in this manner until the engine seized. While the crew worked to extinguish the fire, the vessel grounded and started flooding, which led to the pirate leader cutting the ears of a senior crewmember as punishment and then putting him in solitary confinement for six months. The remaining seafarers were beaten with rods and wires while they tried to remove the water from the engine room manually.

Other reported abuses included systematic physical isolation and deprivation including being forced to stand on deck in the sun without any water, kneeling on the hot deck plates causing second degree burns, being crammed together in a small cabin without ventilation on a hot day, being tied up and kept isolated, and being removed from the ship and taken ashore. Other reported examples of serious abuse included one crewmember's fingers being squeezed with pliers, seafarers being hung overboard and immersed in the sea up to their shoulders, and some even being taken by boat a few miles away from the main vessel, thrown overboard, and abandoned in the water for a period of time.

In addition to these forms of abuse, there were reports of serious and lasting injuries. Seafarers aboard these ships reported incidents including a crewmember being shot in the knee by pirates after an argument about drinking water while pirates stabbed another seafarer in the leg and shot off another crewmember's finger. Another captured crewmember died of an apparent heart attack, which was likely brought on in part by the stress he suffered in captivity.

Psychological Abuse

In addition to the physical abuse reported above, pirates inflicted daily discomfort and psychological abuse. These abuses and threats included:

- Telling seafarers that they had no hope because nobody back home cared about them.

- Allowing the seafarers to speak to their families, then taunting them, abusing them, and firing shots into the air while their families were on the line.

- Making the hostages sleep in cramped conditions without privacy.

- Forcing hostages to drink water from cans contaminated by diesel oil, chemicals, or other toxic substances.

- Isolating hostages both on the vessel and, at times, on shore.

- Telling hostages that because negotiations were not going well, the hostages' organs would be cut out and sold on the open market.

- Threatening to slit the seafarers' throats and feed their bodies to the sharks.

The impact of such abuses can be severe: given the duration of captivity experienced by the crews aboard these ships and the lack of external information or communication with the outside world, the psychological abuse inflicted by pirates could have a disproportionate impact. Aboard one of these ships, a crewman died after intentionally jumping overboard.

Seafarers and the families of seafarers who are directly affected by piracy may suffer a variety of long-term effects even after the active elements of the event are over.

Fatalities

The reports available on seafarer deaths associated with piracy are more comprehensive than the reports of abuse. The number of seafarer and hostage deaths declined in rough proportion to the overall drop in piracy attacks in 2012. As in 2011, the greatest number of fatalities occurred during rescue operations. Two seafarers were killed while they were being used as human shields by the pirates, and another died afterwards due to the severity of his gunshot wounds. Two additional hostages died during their periods of captivity.

The majority of fatalities in 2011 and 2012 occurred during rescue attempts when hostages were used as human shields. One seafarer described the experience of being used as a human shield during a rescue operation:

I was the first one that the pirates picked up to stand up outside. I thought all the while I was going to be used as example and they are going to shoot me in the head. A pirate pointed a .45 caliber at my head, when they brought me in the door of the bridge ... [I thought] they would shoot me while the navy is watching. I was shocked, very shocked at that time. I was so scared as they picked me up ... we were made to stand up on each side of the wings and you can see the bullets [from the navy] coming ... flying towards us.

Interviewer: *Do you think the navy saw you, the crew, standing on the wings of the bridge and that they never stopped shooting?*

Respondent: *No, they never stopped firing.*

The dangers faced by seafarers during rescue operations indicate a high level of risk associated with firefights between pirates and naval vessels due to the willingness of pirates to put seafarers in harm's way. Some seafarers were distressed at the apparent lack of concern for their safety during some rescue attempts. Recalling one such rescue operation, an interviewed seafarer directed his anger at the naval forces rather than the pirates, saying: "What they did was terrible and wrong when the navy attacked our vessel. We may have been much more thankful if the pirates brought us to Somalia and they pay the ransom. No one could have been killed from our crew." . . .

Long-Term Impacts

The impacts of piracy do not end when the attackers stop firing or the hostages are released. Seafarers and the families of seafarers who are directly affected by piracy may suffer a variety of long-term effects even after the active elements of the event are over. The decline in Somali piracy is a heartening trend, but even if all new instances of piracy were to stop tomorrow there would be a large number of seafarers who are still dealing with the impact of past pirate attacks. . . . The rates of long-term distress are difficult to quantify, but if even a small percentage of the thousands of seafarers who have been attacked and held hostage off Somalia showed lasting problems, this would translate to a large number of people who are still dealing with the effects of piracy.

3

Piracy Is Linked with Terrorism in Somalia

Kathryn H. Floyd

Kathryn H. Floyd, a researcher on international conflict and a consultant on strategic communications, also teaches at the College of William and Mary in Williamsburg, Virginia.

The people of the coastal African nation of Somalia live in a country where Islamic militants fight for political control of land and pirates seek to control the sea. Piracy and Islamic militancy developed as parallel trends in Somalia following the collapse of the dictatorship of Mohamed Siad Barre in 1991. When the Somali navy failed to prevent illegal fishing in coastal waters, local fishermen took over this role and eventually turned to more lucrative piracy endeavors. During the same time period, a young militant Islamic movement called al-Shabaab began to challenge the transitional government for political control. Both pirates and militants typically are in their twenties and thirties; are trained to fight with military weapons like AK-47s and rocket-propelled grenades; and are part of an organized, hierarchical command structure. Pirates, however, project power in Somalia by using ransom funds to support entire coastal towns, while al-Shabaab uses fear and violence to gain control over territory. The international community should be concerned about the possibility of either of these groups becoming the governing force in Somalia.

On the eve of the 2009 inauguration of U.S. President Barack Hussein Obama, the biggest terrorist threat to the ceremony did not come from [terrorist organization] al-Qaeda, it emanated from the Somali insurgent group Al-Shabaab. More than two decades have passed since Americans worried about the instability coming from the Horn of Africa, horrified with the images of American soldiers being dragged through the streets of Mogadishu [capital of Somalia] in the infamous "Black Hawk Down" incident. Yet today, Americans and the international community are drawn back toward Somalia and her people who fear neither death nor drought as Islamic militants fight for political control and pirates vie to dominate the seas.

Parallel Movements

The evolution of the pirates and Al-Shabaab militants parallel each other in a number of ways. During the dictatorship of Mohamed Siad Barre from 1969 to 1991, Somali commercial fishing developed with the help of international aid and fixed prices for the abundant seafood. Following the collapse of Barre's regime, this promising industry crumbled and the Somali Navy was unable to patrol illegal fishers in their waters. Local fishermen adopted a defensive position to protect valuable marine life and prevent large companies from dumping toxic waste off their coast to little success, gradually turning to the lucrative profession of piracy. Meanwhile, Al-Shabaab began as the youth militant wing of the Islamic Courts Union, a grouping of Sharia [Islamic law] courts, in their struggle to challenge the 2006 Transitional Federal Government by controlling large portions of southern Somalia and key cities. Broken by an Ethiopian offensive later that year, the Islamic Courts splintered into militant factions such as Al-Shabaab. At the same time as the country's government was disintegrating again, piracy was on the rise as several organizations acted as de facto governments.

One key area where Al-Shabaab and the pirates diverge is the extent to which they aim to project power. The Somali pirates are known to expand their area of operations when being squeezed by international or national patrols, increasingly relying on deep sea mother ships as operating hubs. Their ties are international to the extent that some weapons come from abroad and investors buy and sell shares in forthcoming attacks. The return on investment for the seafaring men is local, with ransom money supporting entire towns. In one example, Dr. Anja Shortland of Chatham House analyzes satellite imagery to deduct that pirates are likely contributing to economic and infrastructure development in the Puntland capitals of Garowe and Bosaso. Al-Shabaab uses a local, national, and international campaign of fear to project their ideology. In the towns, Al-Shabaab will establish mobile Sharia courts to try criminals with immediate sentences ranging from an amputated hand to death. Throughout Somalia, they engage in a series of battles to expand their territory and capture Mogadishu. Internationally, Al-Shabaab draws recruits from the United States and conducts coordinated suicide attacks like those in Uganda in July 2010.

Several pirate groups are quite organized and use a hierarchical military command structure with military weapons like AK-47s and rocket-propelled grenades, as does Al-Shabaab.

A great challenge of this generation is how a follower of a revealed religion, like Islam, is living in a world where secular modernity has won, according to Dr. John Harrison, Department of International Security Studies, The College of International Security Affairs, National Defense University. This paradox is playing out to violent consequence in Somalia. Between 2007 and 2009, some 20 young Somalis were recruited from Minneapolis and St. Paul [Minnesota] to return home and join their militant brothers. While being jubilant about waging jihad, one fighter lamented the lack of Starbucks on his Facebook wall. Militants further engage in a form of psychological warfare as they use scissors to correct "unislamic" haircuts on men and check for the use of unholy brassieres on women in the streets. Al-Shabaab, on a number of occasions, has attempted to challenge some of the pirate port towns and arrange a profit sharing agreement in exchange for not instituting strict Islamic law. Religion can be sacrificed for a share of the booty, but thankfully not a caramel macchiato.

Similarities Between Pirates and Insurgents

Whether a young Somali was a pirate or a militant, he has a job, identity, and role in the larger hierarchy. The typical pirate might have been a local fisherman, former military, or with technical skills yet no job. He is in his 20s or early 30s and is able to earn income and experience as a pirate trained on a variety of weapons and navigation technology. The insurgents are roughly the same age, with a few older civil war fighters. Trained in camps with a proper graduation ceremony, they learn to fight and hold a position within the insurgency. This structure is quite important to both groups. Several pirate groups are quite organized and use a hierarchical military command structure with military weapons like AK-47s and rocket-propelled grenades, as does Al-Shabaab.

As 2012 progresses, the international community has every right to be concerned. In its most serious move toward global jihad yet, Al-Shabaab has announced its merger with al-Qaeda through a joint video. In January [2012], Somali pirates lost several of their own during a U.S. SEAL Team 6 operation that successfully rescued an American hostage and another individual. This small setback, however, is but a drop in the water of the $6.9 billion the pirates collected last year in ransom money. The next few months will be critical if the world's nations are to keep insurgents and pirates from being the governing force that Somalis so desperately need.

4

Pirates Should Be Treated as Terrorists

John R. Bolton

John R. Bolton is a former US ambassador to the United Nations; a senior fellow at the American Enterprise Institute of Public Policy Research, a conservative think tank; and author of the book Surrender Is Not an Option: Defending America at the United Nations and Abroad.

Under international law, maritime piracy is considered a crime that must be dealt with through law enforcement measures— criminal due process, trial, and imprisonment. On the other hand, the international community considers terrorism exempt from criminal due process, making it possible for military force to be used. Yet piracy is not a typical crime seen in civil society; rather, Somali pirates are stateless enemies whose actions are having a serious impact on international trade and oil prices. Piracy, therefore, fits more into the war-against-terror framework than into law enforcement. Treating pirates as criminals has constrained the international community's ability to act in self-defense. What is needed is the right to use decisive military force to destroy the pirates' land bases in Somalia—exactly what President Thomas Jefferson did to end the reign of the Barbary pirates in the early 1800s.

The recent October 1, [2011] kidnapping of a handicapped French woman from a Kenyan resort, initially attributed to Somali pirates, was the second such kidnapping in a month. Kenyan authorities now blame al-Shabab, the Somali terrorist group affiliated with al Qaeda.

Under prevailing international law theories, the kidnappings are law enforcement matters, subjecting the culprits to full criminal due process, trial and imprisonment if found guilty. By contrast, characterized as international terrorism, the abductions could be handled much differently, as Anwar al-Awlaki [an al Qaeda terrorist killed in 2011 by a US drone strike] recently found out unpleasantly in Yemen.

But why should we treat the growing menace of Somali piracy differently from terrorism? Numerous sources already indicate that al-Shabab derives revenues from the pirates, or perhaps al-Shabab is engaging in piracy directly. Especially if the line between terrorists and pirates is becoming even further blurred, why not bring piracy to heel? Even in America's infancy, we knew what to do: Where is today's Stephen Decatur [nineteenth-century US naval officer known for his many naval victories]?

Pirate Land Bases Immune

For more than 20 years, Somalia has been a broken country without effective national government. Famine is widespread, and delivering aid is dangerous. Successive [United Nations] Security Council resolutions have recognized that Somalia's pervasive anarchy constitutes a threat to international peace and security, starting in 1992 with Resolution 733's arms embargo and Resolution 794's authorization of American-led military intervention to open channels for humanitarian assistance. Recent council actions, such as Resolution 1816, explicitly link piracy to Somalia's continuing collapse.

The International Maritime Bureau reports a record 266 pirate attacks globally in the first half of 2011 (compared to

196 last year [2010]), with Somali pirates conducting 60 percent. By this summer, they held 22 ships and 464 seafarers hostage. Particularly given the volume of oil cargoes passing through Somali waters, the impact on worldwide insurance rates and oil prices is high and rising.

The pirates have expanded their depredations at sea and on land despite a substantially increased multinational naval presence off Somalia, the use of military force to rescue hostages, and the creative resort to Kenyan jurisdiction to prosecute and incarcerate pirates in a nearby judicial system. But the pirate bases so far remain effectively immune from decisive military force, as both the pirates and the al-Shabab terrorists fully understand.

Force may be unattractive, but piracy's continuing scourge ... is unacceptable. All that is required ... [is] striking militarily against their bases and infrastructure.

The Need for Military Action

Politically and legally, we have allowed the academic excesses of international law theory to constrict our survival instincts. A now-infamous 2008 British Foreign Office directive cautioned against detaining pirates who might claim asylum in Britain to avoid Shariah [Islamic] law in Somalia and such penalties as having hands chopped off or, shockingly for Brits, the death penalty. This malaise also has infected America, masquerading behind the argument that military force is not appropriate against criminal law violators.

But we are not simply considering shoplifting from the corner store. The contemporary expansion of Somali piracy is a far cry from criminal activity within a functioning civil society. Because the Somali pirates are effectively stateless, normal law enforcement techniques will not be sufficient. Military force has always been justifiable against the "common enemies of mankind," or hostis humani generis, such as pirates.

We must break through our theory-induced ennui. Force may be unattractive, but piracy's continuing scourge, especially combined with terrorism and spreading starvation in Somalia, is unacceptable. All that is required, at least for now, is one step up the escalation ladder, striking militarily against their bases and infrastructure. Because pirates act from pecuniary motives rather than terrorist ideology, we must supersize their operating costs. We should have acted before, but failing to act now will simply facilitate piracy's merger with terrorism, making the combination even harder to destroy.

If international law prevents effective self-defense, its theories are morally flawed, not acting to protect innocent maritime crews and passengers. Somali piracy fits far better (although admittedly imperfectly) into the war-against-terror paradigm than into law enforcement. Both, for example, encounter the same crippling evidentiary and procedural constraints when applying criminal-justice rules. It is nonsensical to engage in legal contortions, cramming piracy or terrorism into inappropriate criminal-justice models suitable within civil societies but not the state of nature prevailing in Somalia.

Nor is this a call for pre-emption—the long list of pirate attacks is already far too real. This is classic self-defense, exactly what [US President] Thomas Jefferson did against the Barbary pirates, legitimate then and equally so today.

Obviously, we will not stoop to the pirates' level, thereby corrupting our own integrity and ideals. We should strive mightily to avoid unnecessarily endangering pirate families, but the bases must be destroyed, the hostages and captured ships released and as many pirates as possible apprehended, dispersed or, if necessary, killed in action.

Destroying pirate bases, repeatedly if necessary, may not end piracy, but the lessons and the costs for the pirates will be far higher and clearer than at present.

5

Pirates Are Not Terrorists

Jon Bellish

Jon Bellish is a project officer at the Oceans Beyond Piracy (OBP) project at the One Earth Future (OEF) Foundation, a think tank founded in 2007 to advocate for more effective systems of governance to achieve a world beyond war.

Former US Ambassador to the United Nations John Bolton and others have argued that treating pirates as terrorists instead of criminals would make the fight against piracy easier. In fact, there are some superficial similarities between the two groups, including the fact that both pirates and terrorists in Somalia are nonstate actors acting in ways that threaten the international community. International law, however, is clear, and under the rule of law pirates cannot be considered terrorists because they do not have terrorist motives. Specifically, under international law, terrorists must have an intent to spread fear among a population or to coerce a national or international government to do something or refrain from doing something. This is clearly not the motive of pirates; instead they simply want to make money. Respect for the rule of law is important and it would be wrong to try to mold international law to fit the piracy situation.

While running through my piracy news roundup yesterday morning, I came across [a] . . . piece by Robert Young Pelton of *Somalia Report*. In it, Pelton criticizes a report by Australia's Lowy Institute that deals with the use of privately contracted armed security personnel (PCASP).

I took particular interest in a small tangent within Pelton's piece that reflects an incorrect sentiment that I have seen repeated many times by non-attorneys (and even by some attorneys): that modern pirates should be considered terrorists.

As Pelton's *Somalia Report* piece primarily concerns PCASP, the terrorism issue is only mentioned in a passing parenthetical:

> Pirates are criminals, (never terrorists because that would prevent the payment of ransoms) so it makes sense that a direct response by putting armed guards on ships was the most logical and so far, the most effective response to the pirate attacks.

International law is clear as to the respective motives necessary to make one a terrorist or a pirate, and the facts on the ground suggest that ... pirates are not terrorists.

From this statement, I gather that Mr. Pelton is of the view that a key reason that the global anti-terrorism network has not been brought to bear against Somali pirates is that such an arrangement would force states to "negotiate with terrorists" once the pirates have seized the vessel and taken hostages. He appears to lament this fact. A similar view has been expressed by former U.S. Ambassador to the United Nations John Bolton and others who argue that relaxed rules concerning due process and state sovereignty as they are applied to terrorists would make the piracy fight a much easier one to win.

Pirates Are Not Terrorists Under International Law

The oft-expressed desire to equate pirates with terrorists likely stems from several superficial similarities between the two groups. First, as Ambassador Bolton points out, "the same crippling evidentiary and procedural constraints" apply to both terrorists and pirates. Also, both groups consist of non-state actors operating in a truly international fashion to the detriment of the broader international community. Finally, both groups tend to base their operations in the Middle East/North Africa region.

Yet international law is clear as to the respective motives necessary to make one a terrorist or a pirate, and the facts on the ground suggest that, no matter how convenient it may be from a policy standpoint, pirates are not terrorists.

A terrorist's intent must be to incite mass fear or coerce a government, both purely political motives; a pirate's motive is strictly limited to making money.

Judge Antonio Cassese, presiding over the Appeals Chamber at Special Tribunal for Lebanon, announced last year that a definition of terrorism has emerged under customary international law. Included in this definition is the requirement that the terrorist has "the intent to spread fear among the population (which would generally entail the creation of public danger) or directly or indirectly coerce a national or international authority to take some action, or to refrain from taking it."

Conversely, it is well-documented that, although piratical intent is not limited to the desire to rob, for an act to be considered piratical, it must be committed for private ends. This requirement is explicitly laid out in UNCLOS [United Nations Convention on the Law of the Sea] art. 101 as well as its predecessor, 1958 Geneva Convention on the High Seas.

A terrorist's intent must be to incite mass fear or coerce a government, both purely political motives; a pirate's motive is strictly limited to making money.

In a smart piece here on piracy-law.com couching this definitional issue in terms of a potential defense available to alleged pirates, Roger Phillips rightly notes that although in theory it is possible to have both political and pecuniary motives, the political motive appears absent in Somali pirates, who choose not to attack well-protected ships or kill hostages simply because it would be less profitable to do so. It seems like a stretch to argue that the pirates' *modus operandi* of attacking a privately-owned ship in the middle of the ocean is somehow carried out in order to coerce a government or frighten the public at large by placing them in danger.

Though Roger [Phillips] covered it thoroughly, this definitional point bears repeating because the terrorist theme has gained so much traction in non-legal commentary on the issue of maritime piracy. As tempting as it is to "talk tough" about pirates and the international community's response to piracy by evoking the specter of terrorism, there is very little merit to the claim that the two terms can, at least presently, be used interchangeably to describe Somali pirates or their West African counterparts.

Respect for the rule of law—apart from being perennial advice given by developed countries to countries like Somalia—requires taking the law as it is written (or trying to change it through legitimate processes) rather than molding it to fit one's immediate policy preferences. Unless evidence of pirates taking a less profitable course in favor of a strategy with large political payoff emerges—or the definitions of piracy and/or terrorism change—the "pirates as terrorists" slogan will continue to be just that—a slogan.

6

The International Multilateral Effort to Combat Piracy Has Succeeded

Andrew J. Shapiro

Andrew J. Shapiro is a former assistant secretary of state at the Bureau of Political-Military Affairs, part of the US Department of State.

In 2009, Somali piracy was out of control but as a result of the efforts of the United States, the international community, and the private sector, pirate attacks decreased significantly in 2012. Pirates are much less successful in staging attacks on ships, and the result is fewer hostages. These gains have been achieved due to a multi-dimensional response by President Barack Obama's administration. This response included: (1) organizing and leading an international effort through the establishment of the Contact Group on Piracy off the Coast of Somalia; (2) encouraging private shipping companies to protect themselves by increasing ship speeds, erecting physical barriers, and hiring armed guards; and (3) efforts to apprehend, prosecute, and incarcerate pirates. A long-term solution to piracy, however, will require a stable government in Somalia—a goal that has partially been achieved through the creation of a new constitution and government in Somalia in 2012. Much work remains, but the United States will stay vigilant in the future.

Andrew J. Shapiro, "Statement Before the House Committee on Transportation and Infrastructure's Subcommittee on Coast Guard and Maritime Transportation," US Department of State, April 10, 2013.

As a maritime nation we rely on the unhindered use of the oceans to ensure our economic well-being, our national defense, and the safety of our fellow citizens wherever they travel. Moreover, we seek to ensure the same for all nations. That the world is a better place when its oceans are available for use by all has been a basic tenet of American policy since the earliest days of our nation and remains a focus for our government today.

Signs of Progress

When I first started this job in the summer of 2009, Somali piracy was spiraling out of control. Attacks were escalating and pirates were expanding operations far into the Indian Ocean. Ransom payments in the millions brought more and more Somali men to the water. When my Principal Deputy last spoke to this sub-committee two years ago [2011], Somali pirates held nearly 600 mariners hostage and pirates roamed an area as large as the continental United States in their search for new victims. In addition to the threat posed to innocent mariners, pirate activity was costing the global economy an estimated $7 billion a year.

Piracy emanating from Somalia represented a perfect storm for the international community—a weak state in a strategically essential location, harboring a rapidly growing transnational criminal enterprise that threatened a vital artery of the global economy. Action *had* to be taken. This prompted Secretary [of State Hillary] Clinton in 2010 to call for a new strategy aimed at tackling pirate networks and to put pirates out of business. And now—after years of hard work, building a novel international forum and pursuing innovative policies and partnerships—successful pirate attacks have plummeted.

While there seemed to be no limit to the growth of piracy, through the collective effort of the United States, the international community, and the private sector, we are now seeing signs of *clear progress*. The numbers tell the story. According to figures from the U.S. Navy, we experienced a 75 percent decline in overall pirate attacks in 2012 compared with 2011. Independent, non-governmental sources, such as the International Maritime Bureau, also indicate a dramatic drop in attacks.

We are seeing fewer attempted attacks in no small measure because pirates are increasingly less successful at hijacking ships. For example, in 2012, pirates captured just ten vessels, compared to 34 in 2011 and 68 in 2010. Remarkably, the last successful Somali pirate attack on a large commercial vessel was on May 10, 2012,—nearly one year ago.

Pirates today can no longer find helpless victims like they could in the past and pirates operating at sea now often operate at a loss.

The lack of success at sea, means that Somali pirates are holding fewer and fewer hostages. In January 2011, pirates held 31 ships and 710 hostages. Today [2013], Somali pirates hold hostage two ships and 60 mariners. That is a more than 90 percent reduction in hostages held by pirates since January 2011. While having just one hostage is still unacceptable, the trend is clear.

Now let me be clear—piracy remains a threat. Pirates at sea are still searching for ships to target as we speak. But while the threat remains, the progress that has been made is real and remarkable.

The U.S. and International Approach to Piracy

I would like to briefly outline our approach to tackling piracy off the coast of Somalia.

The [Barack] Obama administration developed and pursued an integrated multi-dimensional approach to combat piracy. The overriding objective of which, was to make sure that piracy didn't pay. Piracy above all is a business. It is based on the potential to make money by preying on the vast supply of ships that pass through the waters off Somalia. What we have done is made it so the pirate's business model was no longer profitable. Pirates today can no longer find helpless victims like they could in the past and pirates operating at sea now often operate at a loss.

This has truly been an international and an inter-agency effort. I will let my colleagues speak in more detail about the remarkable international naval effort off the coast of Somalia, which has been a critical component of our efforts to combating piracy. The naval effort has helped create a protected transit corridor and has helped ships in need and deterred pirate attacks. However, there is often just too much water to patrol. While naval patrols are an absolutely essential component of any effective counter-piracy strategy, we recognized that we needed to broaden our efforts.

First, the United States has helped lead the international response and galvanize international action. As the State Department's Quadrennial Diplomacy and Development Review concluded, "solving foreign policy problems today requires us to . . . bring countries and peoples together as only America can." This is exactly what the United States has done when addressing the problem of piracy.

All countries connected to the global economy have an interest in addressing piracy. And at a time when the United States was engaged in two wars, this was not a challenge that should simply have fallen on our shoulders alone. We therefore sought to make this a collective effort and build new kinds of partnerships and coalitions.

In January 2009, the United States helped establish the Contact Group on Piracy off the Coast of Somalia, which now includes over 80 nations, and international and industry organizations bound together on an ad hoc and purely voluntary basis. The Contact Group meets frequently to coordinate national and international counter-piracy actions. The Contact Group has become an essential forum. It helps galvanize action and coordinate the counter-piracy efforts of states, as well as regional and international organizations. Through the Contact Group, the international community has been able to coordinate multi-national naval patrols, work through the legal difficulties involved in addressing piracy, and cooperate to impede the financial flows of pirate networks. While we don't always agree on everything at the Contact Group, we agree on a lot, and this coordinated international engagement has spawned considerable international action and leveraged resources and capabilities.

The use of armed security teams has been a game changer *in the effort to combat piracy. To date, not a single ship with armed security personnel aboard has been successfully pirated.*

Second, the United States has sought to empower the private sector to take steps to protect themselves from attack. This has been perhaps the most significant factor in the decline of successful pirate attacks and here too our diplomatic efforts have played a critical role.

We have pushed the maritime industry to adopt so-called Best Management Practices—which include practical measures, such as: proceeding at full-speed through high risk areas and erecting physical barriers, such as razor wire. The U.S. government has required U.S.-flagged vessels sailing in designated high-risk waters to fully implement these measures. These measures have helped harden merchant ships against pirate attack.

But perhaps the ultimate security measure a commercial ship can adopt is the use of privately contracted armed security teams. These teams are often made up of former members of various armed forces, who embark on merchant ships and guard them during transits through high risk waters. The use of armed security teams has been a *game changer* in the effort to combat piracy. To date, *not a single ship* with armed security personnel aboard has been successfully pirated.

For our part, the U.S. government led by example. Early on in the crisis we permitted armed personnel aboard U.S.-flagged merchant vessels in situations where the risk of piracy made it appropriate to do so. We also made a concerted diplomatic effort to encourage port states to permit the transit of armed security teams. This included working with countries to address the varying national legal regimes, which can complicate the movement of these teams and their weapons from ship-to-ship or ship-to-shore. American Ambassadors, Embassy officials, and members of our counter-piracy office at the State Department pressed countries on this issue. I myself, in meetings with senior officials from key maritime states have made the case that permitting armed personnel aboard ships is an effective way to reduce successful incidents of piracy. U.S. diplomatic efforts have therefore been critical to enabling the expanded use of armed personnel.

Third, we have sought to deter piracy through effective apprehension, prosecution and incarceration of pirates and their networks. Today, over 1,000 pirates are in custody in 20 countries around the world. Most are, or will be, convicted and sentenced to lengthy prison terms. The United States has encouraged countries to prosecute pirates and we have supported efforts to increase prison capacity in Somalia. We have also sought to develop a framework for prisoner transfers so convicted pirates serve their sentence back in their home country of Somalia.

But as piracy evolved into an organized transnational criminal enterprise, it became increasingly clear that prosecuting low-level pirates at sea was not on its own going to significantly change the dynamic. We also needed to target pirate kingpins and pirate networks. As any investigator who works organized crime will tell you—we need to follow the money.

This focus is paying off. Today, we are collaborating with law enforcement and the intelligence community, as well as our international partners like Interpol, to detect, track, disrupt, and interdict illicit financial transactions connected to piracy and the criminal networks that finance piracy. We have also helped support the creation of the Regional Anti-Piracy Prosecution and Coordination Center in the Seychelles. This Center hosts multinational law enforcement and intelligence personnel who work together to produce evidentiary packages that can be handed off to any prosecuting authority in a position to bring charges against mid-level and top-tier pirates.

The comprehensive, multilateral approach that we have pursued has helped turn the tide on piracy and has provided an example of how the ... international community can respond to transnational threats and challenges in the future.

This is having an impact. A number of Somali pirate leaders have publicly announced their "retirement" or otherwise declared their intention to get out of the business. Needless to say we and our international partners remain committed to apprehending and convicting these pirate leaders. But it does show they are feeling the impact of our efforts.

Lastly, the most durable long-term solution to piracy is the re-establishment of stability in Somalia. The successful Somali political transition in 2012 that put in place a new provisional constitution, new parliament, and a new president is clearly a step in the right direction, but much remains to be done. Supporting the emergence of effective and responsible governance in Somalia will require continued, accountable assistance to the Somali government to build its capacity to deal with the social, legal, economic, and operational challenges it faces. Once Somalia is capable of policing its own territory and its own waters, piracy will fade away. To that end, the United States continues to support the newly established government in Mogadishu [capital of Somalia].

Staying Vigilant

The comprehensive, multilateral approach that we have pursued has helped turn the tide on piracy and has provided an example of how the U.S. government and the international community can respond to transnational threats and challenges in the future. We have made great strides and we need to ensure that those gains are not discarded—only leaving us to fight for them once again. Pirates can easily get back in their skiffs and renew their mayhem. Let us now stay vigilant and let's work to close the book once and for all on Somali piracy.

Before I close I would just note that in recent months we have noted a disturbing increase in the incidence of maritime crime, including piracy and armed robbery at sea, off the coast of West Africa, specifically in the Gulf of Guinea. While in Somalia, we faced an absence of government until the recent successful political transition in 2012, in the Gulf of Guinea the exact opposite holds true. There are many sovereign governments—with varying degrees of capability—but all with their own laws, their own interests. The tools and relationships we built to roll back Somali piracy are not easily transferable to the Gulf of Guinea. Success in West Africa will depend more on the political will of regional governments to take the steps needed to curtail criminal activity. We can support with capacity building efforts and have an impressive list of those efforts underway. But ultimately tackling this challenge will depend on the countries in the region.

7

Somali Pirates Now Protecting Illegal Fishing Ships

Jason Straziuso

Jason Straziuso is an East Africa correspondent for the Associated Press, an American multinational nonprofit news cooperative headquartered in New York City.

International naval patrols and improved security on commercial ships have dramatically reduced the success rate of pirate attacks off the coast of Somalia, but according to a July 2013 report by a United Nations monitoring group, many Somali pirates have found a new source of revenue—providing security for ships conducting illegal fishing operations in Somali waters. Officials estimate that hundreds of foreign ships are illegally fishing in the northern Somali ocean region, many of them from Iran and Yemen, and former pirates help cast fishing nets and shoot at local Somali fishermen to drive away competition. The report also accuses pirates of dealing in drugs, arms, and humans. This new trend is interesting because some Somali piracy began as a defensive response to illegal fishing and toxic waste dumping.

Frustrated by a string of failed hijacking attempts, Somali pirates have turned to a new business model: providing "security" for ships illegally plundering Somalia's fish stocks—the same scourge that launched the Horn of Africa's piracy era eight years ago.

Somali piracy was recently a fearsome trend that saw dozens of ships and hundreds of hostages taken yearly, but the success rate of the maritime hijackers has fallen dramatically over the last year thanks to increased security on ships and more effective international naval patrols.

Somali pirate gangs in search of new revenue are now providing armed protection for ships illegally fishing Somali waters. Erstwhile pirates are also trafficking in arms, drugs and humans, according to a report published this month by the U.N. [United Nations] Monitoring Group on Somalia and Eritrea.

The security services for fishermen bring piracy full circle. Somali pirate attacks were originally a defensive response to illegal fishing and toxic waste dumping off Somalia's coast. Attacks later evolved into a clan-based, ransom-driven business.

Up to 180 illegal Iranian and 300 illegal Yemeni vessels are fishing Puntland [autonomous state in northeastern Somalia] waters, as well as a small number of Chinese, Taiwanese, Korean and European-owned vessels, according to estimates by officials in the northern Somali region of Puntland. International naval officials corroborate the prevalence of Iranian and Yemeni vessels, the U.N. report said.

We are pleased to see the huge reduction in piracy, and yet equally concerned by the reports of increased criminality.

Fishermen in Puntland "have confirmed that the private security teams on board such vessels are normally provided from pools of demobilized Somali pirates and coordinated by a ring of pirate leaders and associated businessmen operating in Puntland, Somaliland, the United Arab Emirates (UAE), Oman, Yemen and Iran," the report said.

The "security" teams help vessels cast nets and open fire on Somali fishermen in order to drive away competition. "The prize is often lucrative and includes large reef and open water catch, notably tuna," the report says.

The nearly 500-page U.N. report also accuses Somalia's government of wide-ranging corruption. In response, Somalia's presidential spokesman said that the report contains "numerous inaccuracies, contradictions and factual gaps."

"We are pleased to see the huge reduction in piracy, and yet equally concerned by the reports of increased criminality. We have much work to do to create legitimate livelihoods and deter Somalis from crime," said presidential spokesman Abdirahman Omar Osman.

Somali piracy has been lucrative. The hijackings of 149 ships between April 2005 and the end of 2012 netted an estimated $315 million to $385 million in ransom payments, according to an April World Bank report.

But fishermen who have participated in piracy might argue that the attacks were merely bringing back money stolen from Somalis. A 2005 British government report estimated that Somalia lost $100 million in 2003–04 alone due to illegal tuna and shrimp fishing in Somali waters.

In Somalia, pirates sometimes refer to themselves as "saviors of the sea."

A piracy expert at the International Maritime Bureau, said the protection racket makes for a "potentially dangerous situation at sea."

"I guess the region has always been rich in this kind of organized crime," said Cyrus Mody. "I think that probably the positive side of all this is it's being highlighted which would hopefully give the government in place now enough movement to try and do something about it with the help of the EU [European Union] and U.N."

Piracy peaked in 2009 and 2010, when 46 and 47 vessels were hijacked respectively, according to the European Union Naval Force. Hijackings dropped to 25 in 2011, five in 2012 and zero so far this year [2013]. Still, Somali pirates netted an estimated $32 million in ransoms last year, the U.N. report said.

One current pirate said he did not know about pirates providing protection to foreign fishing vessels, but he said some pirates are using Yemeni fishermen to smuggle weapons into Puntland.

"That's our current money-making business because ship hijackings have failed," a pirate commander who goes by the name Bile Hussein said by phone from Garacad, a pirate lair in central Somalia. "If you drop one business, you get an idea for another."

8

The Global Piracy Problem
Is Merely Contained

World Maritime News

World Maritime News is an online site that provides news and information about shipping activities and the maritime industry.

Many shipping companies have hired private security companies to protect their ships against pirate attacks, but those who have yet to do so continue to risk paying large ransoms that amount to an illegal tax that affects the entire maritime industry as well as consumers. A recent payment of a $2.6 million ransom payment to Somali pirates who attacked an Algerian cargo ship is a prime example. Somali pirates remain determined to attack any vulnerable ship, so the piracy threat is not over but only temporarily contained. As recently as 2011, pirate attacks cost $170 million in ransom payments as a result of 439 violent attacks, so it is crucial for the shipping industry and the world's nations to stay vigilant in the fight against maritime piracy.

The revelation this week [May 16, 2013] that the owner of an Algerian cargo ship [*MV Blida*] whose crew was held by Somali pirates paid them $2.6 million in ransom is yet another indication that the rewards these denizens reap for their illegal, life-threatening work remain a serious stumbling block to ending maritime organized crime, according to AdvanFort Company President and COO William H. Watson.

"Those ship owners and operators who have still not hired a highly-reputable private maritime security company (PMSC) continue to risk paying what amounts to an illegal tax in support of further organized maritime extortion," Watson noted in a statement. "It is a cost that ends up being borne by all of us."

Watson noted that the *MV Blida*, carrying 17 Algerians, six Ukrainians, two Filipinos, one Jordanian and one Indonesian, was overtaken by a gang of heavily-armed pirates on its way from Oman to Tanzania, with almost all the hostages freed after a bag full of cash was dropped from a plane to the captors.

"The fact that Rear Admiral Bob Tarrant, the Operation Commander of the EU [European Union] Naval Force, has just issued a warning that Somali pirates still remain determined to get out to sea and attack easy targets should be a wake-up call for those still asleep at the helm of security for their companies," Watson added.

"Tarrant's observation that piracy's threat in the Gulf of Aden and elsewhere is not over, but is merely contained for now, means that the costs associated with world-wide shipping remain burdened by a transnational security threat that carries with it an unnecessary tax that unfairly buffets the maritime industry and those consumers whose life depends on the free flow of commerce."

Although the Gulf of Aden and the Indian Ocean are now protected by a coalition of world navies, in 2011 pirates staged 439 violent attacks and held hostage 802 crewmembers.

"The silver lining in all those clouds on the horizon is the fact that those vessels protected by first-rate PMSCs remain outside the pirates' greedy reach," Watson said.

Piracy Merely Contained

Rear Admiral Tarrant's warning was issued after the EU Naval Force warship *ESPS Rayo* located a skiff with six men on board that was 320 nautical miles off the Somali coast. That the small, open-top boat was so far out to sea caused the *Rayo* to send a team to investigate.

As a result Tarrant said that he was "very concerned that seafarers and nations will lower their guard and support for counter piracy operations in the belief that the piracy threat is over. It is not; it is merely contained. We should remember that at its height in January 2011, 32 ships were pirated by Somali pirates and 736 hostages were held. It is crucial that we remain vigilant or the number of attacks will once again rise."

Although the Gulf of Aden and the Indian Ocean are now protected by a coalition of world navies, in 2011 pirates staged 439 violent attacks and held hostage 802 crewmembers. Although the ransom paid by the Saudi owner of the *MV Blida* was $2.6 million, the average paid to pirates that year was $4.97 million.

According to a recent report, the some $170 million in ransom payments to piracy made during 2011 was a more than 50 percent increase from the total of $110 million they received in 2010. During the period 2007–2011, it noted, the ransoms paid "have increased sevenfold," with average ransoms increasing from about $600,000 in 2007 to some $5 million in 2011.

In February 2011, $13.5 million in ransom was paid to secure the release of a supertanker, the *MV Irene*, which carried 2 million barrels of Kuwaiti oil, estimated to be worth $200 million and destined for the United States.

9

The World Is No Closer to Solving the Piracy Problem

gCaptain

gCaptain is a maritime and offshore industry blog founded by John Konrad, a coauthor of Fire on the Horizon: The Untold Story of the Gulf Oil Disaster, *a 2011 book that details the story of the 2010* Deepwater Horizon *disaster in the Gulf of Mexico.*

Although the number of successful pirate attacks near Somalia declined in 2012, the number of attempted attacks increased, suggesting that the world is no closer to solving the piracy problem. Shipowners want an easy solution but instead see a complex mix of international, diplomatic, and naval anti-piracy efforts as well as private security firms. The US Navy's Maritime Liaison Office (MARLO) therefore has announced that it will seek to increase communication and coordination between political/military efforts in the region and the commerical maritime industry. The goal is to elicit the help and support of shipowners and operators so that government naval forces can better protect commercial ships crossing Somali waters. Private security firms such as Six Maritime, a company based in San Diego, California, are also placing an emphasis on coordinating with naval assets, to help shipowners take advantage of the support available from government antipiracy efforts.

In 2012 the number of successful pirate seizures of merchant ships fell from a 2009 figure of 38 to 21 according to the Combined Maritime Forces (CMF) command in Bahrain but another statistic published by the group highlights a more troubling trend. In an official press release CMF states "The number of attacks, including attempts to seize a vessel, within the HRA [high risk area] has increased from 145 in 2009 to 183 last year."

In short we are no closer to solving the problem, which has only become more complicated since 2009 when Vice Admiral Robert Moeller, former deputy of U.S. Africa Command, referred to piracy near Somalia as "a very, very complex situation."

Since that time the global cost of piracy has steadily increase[d] with current estimates exceeding $7 billion per year as new resources continue to flood the region. Some experts, however, conclude that the addition of coalition warships, diplomatic working groups and private security firms, increases complexity and further confuses ship owners looking for simple solutions.

Connecting Military Support with Ship Operators

For this reason, the U.S. Navy's Maritime Liaison Office (MARLO) recently announced that improving communication and coordination between stakeholders is a top priority for the US Navy. In recent press releases MARLO has stated the need to "coordinate political, military, and other efforts" in the region and to continue its mission to "promote cooperation between the U.S. Navy and the commercial maritime community."

With real time naval intelligence, thousands of Combined Maritime Force (CMF) sailors and dozens of warships available to protect commercial ships transiting Somali waters,

MARLO has a lot of firepower at its disposal. But to be effective they need the help and support of ship owners and operators.

In a recent survey conducted by the maritime industry website gCaptain, only a small percentage of ship operators admitted to taking advantage of naval support, many were unaware of programs (e.g., public intelligence reports, convoys, etc.) and, most surprisingly, some were not aware that naval officers are available at MARLO and CMF to answer their questions. All were confused with some of the options available to them.

Naval support has limited effectiveness unless it is preceded by a close working relationship between ships and naval assets in the region.

Better Communications for Ships

"Private security teams have proven successful in preventing pirates from taking hostages but they are not the only resources available to ship owners," said Joe Allen, CEO of Six Maritime, an American private security company based in San Diego [California].

Six Maritime has taken a unique position in its fight against pirates. Co-founded by Paul A. Robinson, the former head of Research and Development Acquisitions Department at Undersea Naval Special Warfare Group, the company has former Navy S.E.A.L.S [US Navy's special operations force] ready to board ships but the company is, uniquely, focused on helping ships assure they don't have to utilize weapons at sea.

"We have highly trained, combat proven, veterans providing armed security for our clients' assets, but the first order of business when our teams board a client vessel isn't to set up how they are going to fire their weapons at attacking pirates," said Allen. "The first thing they set about doing is making sure the emergency communications procedures are ready so the ship is able to utilize all the resources available to it."

Allen agrees with MARLO on the need to improve communication and coordination between ships and military assets in the region. As a former Navy surface officer himself, Allen knows first hand that naval support has limited effectiveness unless it is preceded by a close working relationship between ships and naval assets in the region. "The Navy will respond to Mayday calls but too often they respond blindly which limits the amount of help they can provide," says Allen. "If a ship wants to be safe and well defended it must help the Navy respond not just during but before an incident takes place."

But with most ships operating with less than two dozen people, a handful of which being English speaking officers trained in maritime security procedures, how will sailors find the time to communicate with naval assets?

Allen and his partners at Six Maritime believe they have the solution. Using a model designed to produce Six Sigma results of success, the company has trained its operators in the use of lethal weapons to a level surpassed by none, but they also place significant emphasis on filing reports, communicating with naval assets and early detection and monitoring of ongoing threats. "We are looking at meeting the needs of shipowners and, in pirate waters, there is a need to provide more than weapons. There is a need to communicate, coordinate, transmit reports and help our clients understand the other assets available to them. Assets, like naval air support, which our clients don't need to pay for."

Joe Allen believes this perspective is both unique and effective but one he is also willing to share with everyone, even ship owners who employ rival security firms.

10

The International Community Must Maintain Its Efforts to Combat Piracy

Sonia Rothwell

Sonia Rothwell is a journalist who specializes in current affairs with a special interest in security issues and international relations.

Pirate attacks off the Horn of Africa have waned in recent years, no doubt because of a variety of antipiracy efforts—naval patrols by the European Union, North Atlantic Treaty Organization (NATO), China, and other countries; shipowner tactics including the use of water hoses and razor wire to deter pirates and create safe rooms for crewmembers; the employment of private security on ships; and land-based solutions such as political changes in Somalia and the establishment of a Somalia-based police force. Yet although piracy has declined in East Africa, there has been an increase in pirate attacks on the West African coast, where pirates steal goods and oil. Also, in such a poor region, the lure of big money from pirate activities is strong and pirates have shown that they can adapt, so the international community must keep up the pressure on piracy to make sure it does not return.

Following its peak between 2005 and 2011, maritime piracy off the Horn of Africa now appears to be abating. The efforts of 40 countries, numerous coalitions and the controversial adoption by some ships of armed guards have contributed to the gradual decrease of both successful and attempted hijackings. But this suggests a far simpler solution to the threat than is the reality. What, for example, are the reasons behind the fall? And with the rise in instances of piracy and robbery in the Gulf of Guinea, West Africa, has the threat simply moved elsewhere?

Money to Be Made

Despite the fact that piracy around the Horn of Africa compromises one of the world's busiest trade routes, the Gulf of Aden, very few studies have attempted to estimate its impact on the global economy. A recently-released report by the World Bank seeks to change that. According to its figures, Somali piracy cost the global economy an estimated $18bn [billion] for the year 2010. The report also notes "that piracy imposes a distortion on trade that has a high absolute cost. When the shortest shipping route between two countries is through piracy-infected waters, the additional cost of trade between them is equivalent to an increase of 0.75 to 1.49 percentage points (with a mean estimate of about 1.1) in total ad valorem trade costs."

But for a poor region largely devoid of structure beyond clan networks, jobs and steady income, the business model for piracy is an attractive one. Somali pirate attacks are long-term investments in that the crews and their backers are prepared to hold out for many months for ransom demands to be met. The outlay is relatively inexpensive at around $80,000 but the ransoms can be lucrative (although payments to financial backers and to communities who tolerate pirate activity can significantly eat into profits, meaning the pirate foot-soldiers may not actually make much money from the risks they take). From such a simple premise, much money has been made. Again, the recent World Bank report estimates that the average ransom in 2011 and 2012 was $4.9m [million].

Sea-Based Solutions

Given such attractive rewards, what are the factors that have contributed to the apparent downturn in fortunes for Somalia's pirate corporations, which have until now shown an impressive ability to adapt their modus operandi? The most visible explanation for the drop in attacks is the increase in international military interest in the region, with the European Union (EU) and NATO [North Atlantic Treaty Organization, an alliance of countries from North America and Europe] among organizations contributing resources to patrolling the vast area of sea in which the pirates operate. Other states, such as China, have also mounted their own operations. Changes in management practices onboard have also helped: boats have better lookouts, simple deterrents such as water hoses and razor wire have been applied and some ships have been equipped with safe rooms (known as citadels) so that crews have somewhere to hide if their vessel is attacked.

Stability on land and the removal of pirate gangs are mutually important if this type of criminal activity is to be curtailed.

The other more controversial move which has been taken by ship-owners is to deploy teams of armed guards on boats. Initial successes prompted the private maritime security industry to stand by the slogan "No ship with armed guards has been hijacked." However, their involvement in counter-piracy operations has raised important questions about states' responsibility for mariners' safety as well as the legal implications of boats carrying arms. Concerns also exist that private security companies have effectively turned vessels into floating armories that may even have the potential to escalate levels of violence.

Nevertheless, the private sector continues to take the fight to the pirates. Glencore, the Swiss-based commodities corporation, has launched its own spin-off private maritime security force, Typhon, to protect the shipment of commodities like cocoa and oil. However, the company is keen to reject any comparisons with the British East India Company [a company chartered by the British government to trade in the East Indies in 1600].

Land-Based Answers

But seaborne measures are not the only tactics which have been applied to stem the number of attacks. Instability on the mainland—Somali piracy, after all, was born in the semi-autonomous state of Puntland—has helped create an ideal environment for criminal activity to thrive. Yet, the political climate in the Horn of Africa is slowly changing. While the writ of Somalia's president Hassan Sheikh Mohamud barely extends beyond Mogadishu [capital of Somalia], the Islamist insurgent group al-Shabab's grip over large swathes of the country continues to come under increased pressure. In 2011, Kenyan troops carried out an incursion into the south of Somalia following a spate of kidnappings of foreigners near the border, apparently by Somali gangs. Around 18,000 African Union troops are also in the country to help contain unrest.

Since it became a significant problem, analysts have routinely said that the solution to Somali piracy is rooted on land. The slow political change currently taking place needs practical if not financial support from richer nations if it is to grow. Problems with accountability in such a lawless state, however, make it difficult to know for certain whether money is being spent in the right areas or is simply ending up in the hands of warlords. But there have been other developments which may have contributed to the drop in attacks.

The development of the apparently UAE [United Arab Emirates]-funded Puntland Maritime Police Force (PMPF) in 2010 to counteract piracy has also been controversial. It is the latest incarnation of a coastguard-type operation charged with reducing the number of pirate attacks. The force is recruited locally but training has been provided by private security firms. It carried out a sweep of pirate villages in 2012 which may have had an impact on the amount of attacks which could be launched. A superficial comparison may be made with the formerly entrenched problem of piracy in the Straits of Malacca. Aceh province, where it is believed many pirates were based, was badly hit by the 2004 tsunami, wiping out many coastal villages. Following the disaster, there was a peace deal between the Free Aceh Movement who had been fighting for 26 years and the Indonesian government.

The pirates have proved on numerous occasions that they are resilient and adaptable ... [so] the international community cannot afford to fall asleep on its watch if the problem is not to return.

Clearly, this is an imperfect comparison. Yet it nevertheless illustrates how stability on land and the removal of pirate gangs are mutually important if this type of criminal activity is to be curtailed. Anecdotally, it also seems that pirates in some areas have made themselves unpopular with the local communities on whose support they depend. Faux pas such as using their newly acquired wealth to take the wives or girl-friends of others have proved unpopular according to one Somali journalist. If this is broadly true, then the pirates have breached [Chinese communist revolutionary] Mao Tse Tung's advice that "the guerrilla must move amongst the people as a fish swims in the sea" thereby working with, and not against, the environment and those within it.

Has Piracy "Gone West?"

But if Somalia's piracy problem has died down somewhat (and there is no guarantee the lull is permanent), piracy on the opposite side of the continent, in the Gulf of Guinea, is rising. Is there a link? In an interview with the author, the International Maritime Bureau (IMB) said the two business models for operations are different; the attacks in the Gulf of Guinea are more often robberies where equipment and possessions are taken, or bunkering operations where oil is siphoned from tankers and sold off elsewhere. There is also a difference onshore with littoral [coastal zone] states such as Nigeria having functioning governments, unlike in Somalia, although that does suggest that law and order is not being adequately maintained. Many of the robberies in the Gulf of Guinea take place within the sovereign waters of the littoral states, meaning that technically they do not count as piracy. And while there is growing support for regional cooperation to bring the problem under control, there is also recognition that legal frameworks are necessary for states to be able to progress on the issue. Recently, for example, a Nigerian naval commander complained that the country lacks the legal frameworks to effectively tackle pirate attacks.

Safeguarding Progress Made

If piracy in the waters around the Horn of Africa is to be contained, current initiatives such as EU Navfor's Operation Atalanta [a military operation by the EU Naval Force to prevent and combat piracy near Somalia] need to be maintained. However, as military budgets are increasingly tightened in the West, it seems increasingly likely that there will have to be a good business case for patrols to be continued. The use of private contractors must also be carefully monitored such is the nervousness about the possible accidental killing of an innocent sailor and the consequences that this and other errors may have on the industry. It also appears that the combination of factors outlined above plus, arguably, jail terms for those who are actually convicted for this notoriously tricky offence to prosecute, have all helped bring down the number of attacks and hijackings. But the pirates have proved on numerous occasions that they are resilient and adaptable. Consequently, the international community cannot afford to fall asleep on its watch if the problem is not to return.

11

The Next Step
Should Be Prosecuting
Major Pirate Kingpins

Damien McElroy

Damien McElroy is a foreign affairs correspondent for The Telegraph, *a daily newspaper published in London and distributed
throughout the United Kingdom and internationally.*

*Piracy has posed a major threat to world trade in recent years,
but naval patrols from the United States, Europe, and Asia have
helped to significantly reduce pirate attacks. Now US State Department officials have said that the United States and its allies
intend to employ a strategy of targeting twelve main pirate kingpins under corruption and money laundering laws with the goal
of defeating the piracy threat within the next two years. The
United States is also using diplomacy to convince countries such
as Panama and the Bahamas to prosecute and imprison pirates.
Already, about one thousand pirates have been sent to prisons in
twenty different countries, and there are donors who plan to
build prisons in Somalia that can be run by the Somalian government.*

Thomas Kelly, the US State Department official in charge
of counter-piracy policy, told *The Daily Telegraph* a small
group of very wealthy men were instrumental in the growth
and spread of Somalian piracy.

Mr Kelly's campaign to prosecute the men under corruption and money laundering laws could be the *coup de grâce* against pirates that at one point represented the gravest threat to world trade in decades.

"That's how we got Al Capone, he went to jail because of tax fraud. One of the main areas of multilateral work and in places like Interpol is to try to focus on the kingpins," he said. "Just incarcerating young Somali men who are the foot soldiers isn't going to eradicate the problem by itself."

The overall economic cost to the world economy inflicted by Somalia piracy was estimated as $12 billion (£7.5 billion) in 2010 alone.

With global backing, all of the men could be facing the courts within the next "couple of years," he added.

"You have to go after the people who are buying the boats, buying the weapons and then laundering the money in Africa and other places. Money laundering is a global business; they're not keeping it in one place you need to have law enforcement in many different places talking to each other."

Somalia's Biggest Industry

Piracy became Somalia's biggest industry as warlords moved off shore to intercept oil tankers and container ships that were then ransomed for as much as £7 million [roughly $11 million] a ship.

Taking into account higher insurance premiums and other costs to shipping firms, the overall economic cost to the world economy inflicted by Somalia piracy was estimated as $12 billion (£7.5 billion) in 2010 alone.

Figures released by the International Maritime Organisation show a dramatic drop in piracy this year [2012]. It catalogued just 70 incidents in the first nine months, a 75 per cent fall off from the same period in 2011 and a three year low.

Mr Kelly said that the combination of increased patrolling by navies from the US, Europe and Asia as well as the employment of armed guards on ships was a turning point in the battle against piracy.

"There was a lot of reticence in a lot of places about using these crews but people learned through experience that this was a critically important factor in reducing the number of instances," Mr Kelly said. "Its hard enough to climb up the side of a ship with a Kalashnikov [assault rifle] on your back but it's harder when you have someone shooting down at you."

Four fifths of container ships and tankers now carry armed guards, leaving pirates with fewer targets to go after.

"Pirates break off attack and look for softer targets," he said. "We estimate 80 per cent of ships are using private security. We'd like it to be 100 per cent."

America is also mounting a diplomatic campaign to share the burden of imprisoned pirates with countries that dominate the registry of shipping. Countries such as Panama and the Bahamas are being asked to prosecute and imprison pirates caught on their vessels.

About 1,000 pirates have been imprisoned in 20 nations as a result of the crackdown on the trade. An international conference on Somalia in London in January [2012] backed a British-financed initiative to stage trials of pirates in the Seychelles. Kenyan courts have also sentenced hundreds of pirates to prison.

In the long run, foreign donors plan to build prisons run by the fledging government of Somalia to house the country's pirates.

12

Investments in Technology Could Help Solve the Piracy Problem

Crispin Andrews

Crispin Andrews is a freelance writer and journalist based in the United Kingdom.

Piracy on Africa's East Coast is on the decline but on the West Coast of Africa it is getting worse, often involving attacks against oil tankers. Some coastal countries in West Africa have the ability to police their seas, but others lack the resources to effectively deal with the new pirate threat. However, technology could be employed to help West African nations locate pirates both at sea and on land without funding expensive patrol forces. Sensor networks such as the Automatic Identification System (AIS), for example, can help track boats believed to be carrying weapons or stolen oil within sovereign waters, and satellite technology can show areas on land where rapid development might mean the influx of piracy funds. Technological solutions such as these will not completely solve the piracy problem but it is important to educate African countries about technology so that it can be employed in the fight against piracy. At the same time, African governments must deal with social issues, such as why young men turn to piracy and why local cultures celebrate it instead of condemning it.

Crispin Andrews, "Technology Versus Piracy," *Engineering and Technology Magazine*, vol. 8, no. 5, June 2013, pp. 44–47. Copyright © 2013 by The IET. All rights reserved. Reproduced by permission.

Piracy in much of Africa is on the decline, yet on the continent's west coast it seems to be getting worse. Solving this problem will take a concerted international effort in the fields of technology and social development. Last January [2013], Somali crime lord Mohamed Abdi Hassan announced that he no longer wanted to be a pirate. After eight years of hijacking ships, stealing cargo and ransoming hostages in the Gulf of Aden and the Indian Ocean, Hassan, or 'Big Mouth' as he's known, said he was giving it all up. Also, that he'd persuaded many of his pirate comrades to do the same.

Hassan didn't explain why, but his decision coincides with a significant drop in reported incidents of piracy off Africa's East Coast. Since 1991, Somalia has been ravaged by civil war and conflict. The lack of a single effective central authority has allowed pirate gangs, extremist militia and other armed groups to control mini-fiefdoms in northern and southern parts of the country. Piracy around Somalia got so bad, that in October 2008, a UN [United Nations] resolution, backed by what's left of the Somali government, allowed countries with commercial vessels in the area to send warships to patrol the seas. Many commercial ships also employ armed guards to ward off pirate attacks and put barbed wire around the hoardings to make it more difficult for raiders to board.

Somali pirates still attack ships as far east as the Seychelles and the Maldives and as far south as the Mozambique Channel. Whereas in 2009, they managed to seize one in every three ships they targeted, now it's more like one in 20. Between January and September 2011 there were 199 raids. Last year, there were 70 attacks during those same months and only one in July and August compared to 36 the previous year.

On the West Coast of Africa, however, piracy is getting worse. Here, there is no UN resolution and no patrolling foreign warships to deter pirates. Governments insist that commercial ships employ local security firms—a problem when a ship has to travel through more than one nation's seas to get to their destination. Some ships break the protocols and arm their own guards, who then dump weapons overboard before they get to port. However, many companies won't take the risk. The authorities in that part of the world police these rules strictly; a problem that pirates use to their advantage.

Last July [2012], there were 32 reports of hijackings in the Gulf of Guinea, 17 of which were in Nigerian waters. In October, seven foreigners working for French oil transport company Bourbon were kidnapped while boarding a vessel belonging to the company on Nigeria's Pennington River. This February [2013] there were five pirate attacks in Nigerian waters. Around the same time, pirates hijacked several oil tankers off the Ivory Coast.

Sensor networks . . . can help authorities track vessels suspected of carrying illegal weapons or stolen oil within about 20 nautical miles from the coast.

Security Needs Technology

"Pirates will pay off people in docks and aboard ships to 'lose' cargo," says Augustus Vogel, associate director at the US Department of Defense's Office of Naval Research Global. He explains that they'll also damage pipelines and siphon off the oil, and as they seldom stick to one country's seas, they are hard to find.

While some countries, such as Nigeria, have a maritime security presence, others don't. "Many African countries prioritise investment in land-based forces over maritime units, rendering surveillance beyond coastal observation all but impossible," Vogel says. He explains that maritime policing and management require the sort of cross-national cooperation that is difficult to achieve. "Some countries supposedly have agreements to chase people across borders, but many don't."

In West Africa, security needs technology. The problem is that the pirates are not easy to find. They don't fly the Jolly Roger [a pirate flag] and wear wooden legs. From a distance, these people look like fishermen. Most often there's a few of them, in small to medium-sized speedboats. Any guns, grappling hooks and boarding ladders will be well out of sight. Even satellites would not necessarily pick out who the pirates are.

Vogel explains that sensor networks such as Automatic Identification System (AIS) towers can help authorities track vessels suspected of carrying illegal weapons or stolen oil within about 20 nautical miles from the coast. "You don't get a complete surveillance picture because not all ships carry transponders and towers are limited by line of sight," he says. "It is much cheaper than relying solely on patrol boats, though, which cost thousands of dollars per day to operate."

Quinsec Solutions

John Holden, managing director of maritime security company Quinsec, adds that the intelligence picture in the Gulf of Guinea is a bit ad hoc. He explains that information the International Maritime Bureau and UK [United Kingdom] Maritime Trade Operation disseminate to ships in the high risk area is only as good as the information the organisations themselves receive. "Our research indicates that suspicious vessel sightings, or even attacks, often go unreported," Holden says. "It's important to report attacks and suspicious activity as quickly and accurately as possible, so that all ships operating in the area have an idea where potential pirates might be. Armed with this information, ships can change speed, re-route if necessary, and security services can dispatch responders to deal with threats."

Holden hopes Quinsec's new maritime security system will provide this type of support. It consists of two portable cameras with infrared night vision, motion detection, snap-shot ability and audio record capability. These can be moved around a ship to monitor potential threats. "The cameras are linked to satellite systems," Holden says. "In the event of a suspicious sighting or attack, audio and images are relayed to our 24-hour operations room and sent on to other ships and the authorities."

One of the first things pirates will do when they board a ship is turn off the vessel's navigational systems and location devices. Quinsec hides their tracking device so not even the crew know where it is. "If the device is found and switched off, it automatically alerts our 24-hour operation HQ [headquarters], which immediately begins tracking the vessel," Holden says.

The tracking device also uses satellite technology which sends alerts if a vessel enters a prohibited area, goes off course or changes speed unexpectedly. The Quinsec system provides a 360-degree image of the ship's exterior and interior, integrated with ships' plans. Should a ship get hijacked, this knowledge makes it easier for a Special Forces team to plan a rescue attempt.

Satellite technology could help take the fight against the Somali pirates inland.

Warships and armed guards haven't completely solved the piracy problem in East Africa. Experts warn that Somali pirates, such as Mohamed Abdi Hassan, might not have hung up their grappling hooks for good. More likely that they are biding their time.

"The apparatus of the pirates onshore has not been dismantled," says Stig Jarle Hansen, an African security expert from the Norwegian University of Life Sciences. "As soon as there is any sign of a lack of continued interest by the international community, this thing will come back."

Poverty Leads to Piracy

Piracy in Africa is driven by local social and economic realities. Even if the Somali government eventually takes control of the whole country; the average wage will still be around $300 a year. Ransoms for single pirate hijacks ranged from US$690,000 to US$3m [million] in 2008 but climbed to a record US$9m in 2010. In 2008, the United Nations estimated that 40 per cent of the proceeds of piracy directly funds local employment. There are also as yet unproven accusations that pirates fund the militant Islamic group al-Shabaab.

Simply throwing technology at either East or West Africa will [not] solve the piracy problem. . . . [But] helping key people within African states gain a realistic understanding of what the technology can do is the way forward.

Research carried out by UK international affairs analysts, Chatham House, suggests that satellite technology could help take the fight against the Somali pirates inland. The researchers compared high-resolution satellite maps and nightlight emissions from Puntland, a semi-autonomous region within Somalia and the main pirate haven. The researchers looked at maps from 2002, before most of the pirate activity began, and 2009. It wasn't quite a treasure map, but researchers believe that certain parts of Somalia have undergone rapid development that coincides with the time pirates have been active in the area. The researchers can't be sure that this development was funded by piracy, but in an area that is not exactly booming financially, they think this is the most likely explanation.

The Chatham House report, released in 2010, shows that between February 2002 and July 2009 Garowe, Puntland's capital, almost doubled in size. Significant housing, light industrial and commercial developments went up in the south-east and south of the town. Researchers also noticed a substantial increase in traffic and several new hotels catering for wealthy clients.

In the 2002 image there were few cars parked outside residential buildings whereas in the 2009 image there are lots, mostly outside new houses with security walls. Pirates often boast of buying cars and houses with their proceeds. Nighttime satellite images show that since 2007, while the rest of the country was getting darker as people couldn't afford electricity, Garowe and Bosaso, Puntland's largest city, were brighter than ever. The Chatham House researchers concluded that pirates appeared to be investing money in the main cities, not the coastal communities where the pirate activity takes place. Many pirate gangs recruit gunmen and support teams from inland but employ local fishermen to pilot their attack craft. The report's author, Dr Anja Shortland from Brunei University, thinks it may be possible to turn coastal communities against the pirates. "A negotiated solution to the piracy problem should aim to exploit local disappointment among coastal communities . . . and offer them an alternative," she says.

Technology Is Not Enough

Vogel isn't convinced that simply throwing technology at either East or West Africa will solve the piracy problem. He believes that helping key people within African states gain a realistic understanding of what the technology can do is the way forward.

"Some people think that you will give them this technology and it will magically show them where all the pirates are," he says. "It's important to understand what kind of benefits technology can bring, not to over estimate what it might do." Investment in the science half of science and technology, Vogel believes, is essential if the benefits of technology are to be fully realised and sustained.

"Without it, there is no one to manage the installed technology and analyse the data generated," he says, explaining that in many cases where AIS towers have been installed in Africa, international partners must provide even basic repairs. "African governments have rarely linked their towers through the Internet to develop a comprehensive operating picture—the ultimate aim of this surveillance network," Vogel adds, explaining that African governments tend to spend more on operations directly responsible for ship-based patrolling, and have not established research and development units for repair strategies, technological development, and long-term maintenance.

He believes that international companies could provide more training in the operation and repair of the equipment that they sell, but that the real way forward is for African governments and militaries to engage with African universities who can provide the missing expertise. Even more important, Vogel believes, is how African governments deal with social situations that fuel piracy as a life choice. Situations where young men turn to piracy, because they have nothing better to do and no other way of getting rich. Also, how to find a solution within cultures, that while they don't openly support or celebrate piracy; neither do they condemn it. "It's like piracy is an accepted part of society," he says. "Rather than criminals, people see pirates as Robin Hood type figures."

Vogel believes that governments working with African universities will help develop a new dialogue within African countries. One that's driven by a generation of locals who are well educated, well-travelled and understand the potential, but also the limitations of the technology they are buying and how best to use it to deal with local issues. "How to monitor the ocean, track ships," he says, "but also how to deal with the societal processes that sustain piracy."

The military mind, however, when dealing with far away places, can be more concerned with immediate impact than long-term solutions. The US navy first deployed MQ-9 Reapers off the East African coast since these drones are apparently unarmed. Last December, UK Defence Minister Philip Dunne said the MOD [UK Ministry of Defense] planned to deploy UAVs [unmanned aerial vehicles] at sea by spring 2013. Could flying drones already be monitoring and getting ready to blow suspected Somalian pirate ships out of the water? That's classified, according to Dunne.

And if a few innocent fishermen are blown to bits along the way? Collateral damage. Not a problem. Not until hundreds more Somalians start joining al-Shabaab, that is.

Tackling Piracy

This April [2013], the MOD commissioned Qinetiq to investigate how the Royal Navy can coordinate the defence of its vessels against attack by small agile boats. They hope to develop new technology that enables commanders to respond more quickly to threats. The technology will combine detection, weapon firing and decision making.

The world's first superactivating watercraft was granted a patent this April. Powered by jet fuel; it is said to be able to travel at speeds in excess of a mile a minute. It travels across water like a boat, but through a tunnel of gas below the surface. Ghost moves through the gas faster than water, which has 900 times more drag. It can carry thousands of kilos of weapons, including torpedoes. It will be able to conduct long range security patrols at high speeds and loiter for several days.

Better security patrols and cooperation between neighbouring countries to secure waterways has reduced piracy in the South China Sea. Last August [2012] there were only six pirate attacks in the area, half as many as the previous year. The Regional Cooperation Agreement on Combating Piracy and Armed Robbery against Ships in Asia (ReCAAP) is the first regional government-to-government agreement to promote and enhance cooperation against piracy and armed robbery in Asia. So far, 18 countries have become contracting parties.

The US Navy has a sophisticated computer model that combines weather, ocean currents, shipping routes and classified intelligence data to predict where pirates may strike next. Naval researchers update the anti-pirate program every 12 hours with new data about winds, wave heights and undersea currents—all factors that affect the pirates' ability to attack commercial ships. The model, known as the Piracy Attack Risk Surface (PARS), also uses classified reports about pirate whereabouts from captured sailors or unmanned drone aircraft patrolling the skies. The result is a colour-coded map that divides an ocean into zones of probability of pirate strikes.

13

Ending Somali Piracy: Go After the System, Not Just the Pirates

The World Bank

The World Bank was founded in 1944 to facilitate post-World War II reconstruction. It has expanded to a group of five development institutions—the International Bank for Reconstruction and Development, the International Development Association, the International Finance Corporation, the Multilateral Investment Guarantee Agency, and the International Centre for the Settlement of Investment Disputes—that seek to alleviate poverty worldwide.

So far, the world has fought Somali piracy with naval forces and by prosecuting pirates, but a new World Bank study proposes that the international community must help Somalia build a stable political system in order to find a permanent solution to the piracy problem. The study found that a history of European colonization and clan infighting has left the country without functional institutions—a situation that allows pirates to recruit unemployed youths, buy equipment, and secure safe havens in coastal villages through bribes and threats. In fact, the study said that up to 86 percent of piracy proceeds go toward these operations. Yet piracy has caused hundreds of deaths of ship crewmembers, billions of dollars of costs to world trade, and harm to local fisheries and tourism. The international community has re-

sponded with offshore actions such as naval patrols and en-hanced ship security but these methods are expensive and unsus-tainable. The study therefore urges world leaders to shift towards onshore efforts such as removing pirates' access to safe anchorage sites or offering incentives to encourage local people and officials to stop pirate activities.

The global fight against piracy in Somalia has centered on prosecuting pirates and mobilizing naval forces. But to get to the root cause of the problem, the international commu-nity must focus on helping the nation build a functional po-litical system, according to a new World Bank study.

"Piracy is a symptom of the breakdown of Somalia's po-litical system," says Quy-Toan Do, a senior economist in the Bank's research department and lead author of the report, "The Pirates of Somalia: Ending the Threat, Rebuilding a Na-tion." "Go after the system, not just the pirates."

Three elements—political capital, manpower and financial resources—form the foundation of the hijack-for-ransom phenomenon in Somalia, where a history of inter- and intra-clan competition and European colonization has left many ar-eas without functioning institutions, according to the study. That has allowed pirates to recruit local youth, buy guns and speedboats, and most importantly, secure coastal areas where they can anchor hijacked vessels for months or years.

Pirates in the East African nation favor places such as Puntland and Central Somalia, which provide enough political stability to do business in, but not enough state control to challenge piracy operations. They then use bribes and physical threats to tilt the balance of power between politicians and gain long-term access to the coasts.

The cost of that political operation takes up as much as 86% of the piracy proceeds, according to the study. A large sum—sometimes $300,000 per vessel—goes to government officials, businessmen, clans, militia and religious leaders as bribes and "development fees" to make sure the politicians won't interfere in the piracy business. Crewmembers, often hired from a particular clan or location, command significantly higher salaries than local wages. Pirates also pay more than locals do for meal services, energy, and water. Given the local custom of resource sharing, piracy proceeds trickle down to local residents and other stakeholders, creating a favorable political environment in which the pirates can operate.

Their success has global consequences. Between 2005 and 2012, more than 3,740 crewmembers from 125 countries fell prey to Somali pirates, and as many as 97 died. On the Somali side, the number of pirates lost at sea is believed to be in the hundreds. The ransom extracted during that period rose to as much as $385 million. Piracy also hurts trade, as shippers are forced to alter trading routes and pay more for fuel and insurance premiums, costing the world economy $18 billion a year, the study estimates. Since 2006, tourism and fish catches, as well as other outputs from coastal commerce, have declined in neighboring countries in East Africa.

Piracy would be less profitable if Somalia removes access to safe anchorage points or significantly raises the price for coastal access.

Somalia's economy is not spared either: piracy-related trade costs are at $6 million a year, without taking into account the fact that potential sea-based economic activities are constrained by piracy. The collaboration between pirates and Islamist insurgent groups also has raised concerns about Somalia's political stability.

The Need for State-Building in Somalia

The international community has mostly focused on offshore measures to fight piracy, such as increasing naval pressure and onboard security, which have helped reduce the number of hijacks. But ending piracy would call for those costly measures to be expanded and made permanent, which wouldn't be sustainable in the long run. Efforts that target onshore prevention, such as paying youth more to discourage them from joining the pirates, would only prompt owners to pay crew members more. Given the poverty rates among the population from which the pirates are typically recruited, owners can afford to pay pirates more without significantly hurting profit.

To end piracy off the Horn of Africa, the study urges a paradigm shift away from perpetrators and toward the enablers of piracy. With a limited number of suitable coastal areas available to anchor hijacked ships, piracy would be less profitable if Somalia removes access to safe anchorage points or significantly raises the price for coastal access. In addition, the central government can offer incentives—along with built-in monitoring mechanisms—to encourage local stakeholders to stop pirate activity and learn from the success and failure of Afghanistan's policies targeting opium poppy production and Colombia's against coca production.

At the heart of this policy agenda lies the need to better understand the political economy of resource sharing, so that winners and losers are properly identified and compensated. The lessons from the study go beyond piracy eradication and speak to the fundamental issue of state building in Somalia.

14

Somalia Is Already Implementing Onshore Tactics to End Piracy Problems

Abdi Moalim

Abdi Moalim reports for Sabahionline.com from Mogadishu, Somalia's capital city. The Sabahi website is sponsored by US Africa Command, the command currently working to support and enhance US efforts to promote stability and cooperation in the region.

In 2013, the Somali government began a new antipiracy campaign to reach out to pirates, offer them employment, and convince them to give up piracy. Also part of the plan is forgiveness for those who quit piracy and releasing others from prisons. Government officials praised a recent World Bank report that called for support for Somalia's government and onshore solutions as the path that will lead to a more permanent solution to the piracy problem. World Bank officials, in turn, offered praise for Somalia's efforts to combat piracy, saying that building a stronger nation that can provide employment and other opportunities to young people is the right course. Somalia, however, also intends to strengthen a coast guard and maritime police force capable of monitoring and policing the seas and coastal areas used by pirates. Already the nation has set up headquarters in areas known to be pirate locations on land and this has led to a reduction in pirate activities at sea.

Abdi Moalim, "Somalia Charts New Course in Battle Against Piracy," Sabahionline.com, April 16, 2013.

Over the past few weeks [April 2013] the Somali government has begun implementing new tactics to combat the longstanding scourge of piracy: starting an anti-piracy outreach campaign and providing employment opportunities for pirates to persuade them to give up crime on the high seas.

Building a Strong Somalia

"Guns alone cannot be used to solve matters, so we started talks with pirates and have convinced some of them to begin new lives and quit that lifestyle," Somali Minister of Natural Resources Abdirizak Omar Mohamed said. "On our part, we have [forgiven] those who quit piracy and have released others from the prisons," he said.

"Creating new employment opportunities is one of the ways that can be used to eliminate piracy," Mohamed told Sabahi [a website sponsored by the US Africa Command]. "However, we need the international community to help us facilitate new lifestyles and income generation for these young people once we succeed in getting them to quit piracy. That is the solution to piracy."

The World Bank on April 11th [2013] published a report dealing with this question and emphasising how continued nation-building in Somalia would help do away with the persistent problem of piracy.

Titled "The Pirates of Somalia: Ending the Threat, Rebuilding a Nation," the 187-page report details how piracy off Somalia and the coasts of neighbouring countries has resulted in humanitarian, financial and natural resource losses.

According to the World Bank, since 2005, 149 hostage situations perpetrated by pirates against ships and other vessels have resulted in 3,741 sailors from 125 countries captured in hijackings. Out of the 149 standoffs, between 82 and 92 casualties were reported and shipping companies were forced to pay an estimated $318–$385 million in ransom money.

"Pirates have imposed an indirect tax on global trade and the estimated yearly cost to the global economy is $18 billion," according to the report. "The average annual amount used to pay ransom since 2005 is $53 million."

The World Bank is calling for international support of Somali government efforts to combat piracy, saying that helping build a strong Somalia is central to solving this issue.

"By better understanding how piracy has been enabled in towns and communities along the Somali coast gives the new government in Mogadishu [capital of Somalia] and the international community a much better idea of the development policies and alliances that will be needed to end piracy in these hotspots and to re-establish a thriving new Somali state in East Africa," Bella Bird, the World Bank's country director for Somalia, Sudan and South Sudan, said in a press release April 11th.

Bird, who is working closely with the Somali government on its plans to provide essential services to the Somali people, said the World Bank would assist the government in creating jobs and other opportunities for Somalis, including pirates.

As the federal government takes a non-military approach to combatting piracy, it should also strengthen Somalia's coast guard and build up a maritime force that pirates would fear.

"I was encouraged by the long term outlook of the Somali government in creating jobs for those who give up piracy, as I believe the cause of piracy has been unemployment and a weak government," Bird told Sabahi.

Mohamed, the minister of natural resources, praised the World Bank report, saying it supports the Somali federal government's approach in fighting piracy.

"The report said the solution to piracy includes outreach with pirates as well as creating opportunities or providing money for them to start self-employment, and that is [also] our view," he said, adding that re-directing a small portion of the more than $1 billion that is spent annually for anti-piracy maritime patrols to rehabilitation programmes could help eliminate piracy altogether.

Fighting Piracy on Two Fronts

As the federal government takes a non-military approach to combatting piracy, it should also strengthen Somalia's coast guard and build up a maritime force that pirates would fear, said Admiral Farah Ahmed Omar Qare, commander of Somalia's navy.

"The law cannot be upheld without a force to fear, hence the pirates have to feel that they can be forcefully taken down if they refuse peace," Qare told Sabahi. "Therefore, we intend to take advantage of the arms embargo that has been lifted from us to arm the marine forces."

"Currently, 400 former pirates have quit piracy and surrendered to the law, and thousands more will potentially surrender if the troops are strengthened," he said.

Admiral Abdirizaq Dirie Farah, who commands the coast guard in the Puntland region, said that stepped-up coastal policing has proven effective.

"We have created headquarters in the locations the pirates use to enter the sea and the places they land when they finish their business, and it has resulted in a reduction of pirate attacks in the sea," Farah told Sabahi. "This programme needs to be strengthened."

Jay Bahadur, a Nairobi-based reporter and author of the book *The Pirates of Somalia: Inside Their Hidden World*, agreed that the Somali government needs to step up efforts to eliminate the threat of piracy.

"The long term solution to eliminate piracy involves a full implementation of the law in the land and the creation of special police units equipped with 4x4 vehicles that are spread out in the regions adjacent to the coast," Bahadur told Sabahi.

"Even though developing the Somali economy is a good goal, I do not believe that creating employment opportunities will be a solution to piracy in the short term," he said.

Organizations to Contact

The editors have compiled the following list of organizations concerned with the issues debated in this book. The descriptions are derived from materials provided by the organizations. All have publications or information available for interested readers. The list was compiled on the date of publication of the present volume; names, addresses, phone and fax numbers, and e-mail and Internet addresses may change. Be aware that many organizations take several weeks or longer to respond to inquiries, so allow as much time as possible.

Cargo Security International (CSI)
Petrospot Limited, Petrospot House, Somerville Court
Trinity Way, Adderbury, Oxfordshire   OX73SN
   United Kingdom
+44 1295 814455 • fax: +44 1295 814466
e-mail: info@cargosecurity.com
website: www.cargosecurityintelligence.com

Cargo Security International (CSI) is a website published by Petrospot Limited, a publishing, training, and events organization that provides information resources for the transportation, energy, and maritime industries. The CSI website provides information and intelligence on security-related commercial and governmental initiatives to transportation and security professionals, including updates on maritime piracy. A bimonthly magazine, *Cargo Security International,* is available on the site and a click on the website's piracy topic leads to numerous articles about this subject. Recent articles include: "Piracy Falls in 2012, But Seas off East and West Africa Remain Dangerous, Says IMB" and "New EU Initiative to Combat Piracy in the Gulf of Guinea".

Contact Group on Piracy off the Coast of Somalia (CGPCS)
e-mail: cgpcs@mofat.go.kr.
website: www.thecgpcs.org

The Contact Group on Piracy off the Coast of Somalia (CGPCS) is a voluntary, ad hoc international forum created on January 14, 2009, pursuant to United Nations (UN) Security Council Resolution 1851. CGPCS brings together countries, organizations, and industry groups to coordinate political, military, and other efforts to bring an end to piracy off the coast of Somalia and to ensure that pirates are prosecuted. Nearly sixty countries and several international organizations participate in the group, including the African Union, the Arab League, the European Union, the International Maritime Organization, the North Atlantic Treaty Organization, and various departments and agencies of the United Nations. The CGPCS website provides news articles, UN documents, legal documents, and reports from other organizations and entities involved in antipiracy work.

Heritage Foundation

214 Massachusetts Ave. NE, Washington, DC   20002-4999
(202) 546-4400
website: www.heritage.org

The Heritage Foundation is a research and educational institution that seeks to promote conservative public policies based on the principles of free enterprise, limited government, individual freedom, traditional American values, and a strong national defense. The group transmits its research and ideas primarily to members of Congress, key congressional staff members, policymakers in the executive branch, the nation's news media, and the academic and policy communities. Searching the website reveals numerous articles and blog postings on the topic of piracy. Examples include "Somaliland: A Reliable Partner in Combating Piracy," "Stopping Piracy Matters," and "The Right Way to Fight Piracy and the Wrong Way to Defend Network Freedom."

ICC International Maritime Bureau (IMB)

ICC Commercial Crime Services, Cinnabar Wharf
26 Wapping High St., London   E1W1NG
   United Kingdom

+44 2074 236960 • fax: +44 2074 236961
e-mail: imb@icc-ccs.org
website: www.icc-ccs.org

The ICC International Maritime Bureau (IMB), a division of the International Chamber of Commerce (ICC), is a nonprofit organization founded to fight against all types of maritime crime. IMB's main goal is to protect the integrity of international trade. The IMB operates the Piracy Reporting Centre (PRC), which tracks actual and attempted pirate attacks worldwide and tries to raise awareness within the shipping industry of the areas and ports of high risk for attacks. The PRC works closely with various governments and law enforcement agencies and is involved in information sharing in an attempt to reduce and ultimately eradicate this piracy. Clicking on the PRC icon on the IMB website provides advice for shipowners, piracy news and data, as well as a weekly piracy report listing specific episodes of piracy.

International Maritime Organization (IMO)

4, Albert Embankment, London   SE17SR
   United Kingdom
+44 2077 357611 • fax: +44 2075 873210
e-mail: MaritimeKnowledgeCentre@imo.org
website: www.imo.org

The International Maritime Organization (IMO) is the United Nations agency responsible for the safety and security of shipping and the prevention of marine pollution by ships. The IMO's Maritime Knowledge Centre maintains collections of publications on various topics, including maritime safety, and clicking on the "Our Work" icon on the IMO website leads to a section on piracy, which contains an introduction to the topic as well as piracy laws, reports, and statistics.

INTERPOL

General Secretariat 200, quai Charles de Gaulle, Lyon   69006
   France

fax: +33 (0)4 72 44 71 63
website: www.interpol.com

INTERPOL is the world's largest international police organization, made up of 188 member countries. It seeks to facilitate international police cooperation in order to prevent or combat various types of international crime. INTERPOL's involvement in the fight against international terrorism includes maritime piracy, and a search of the INTERPOL website leads to various factsheets on INTERPOL's response to piracy, international involvement, and other issues. The site also provides news and media releases on the subject of piracy.

Oceans Beyond Piracy (OBP)
One Earth Future Foundation—OBP Project
525 Zang St., Suite C+D, Broomfield, CO   80021
(720) 266-2552
e-mail: maritimepiracy@oneearthfuture.org
website: http://oceansbeyondpiracy.org

Oceans Beyond Piracy (OBP) is a project of the One Earth Future Foundation, a private nonprofit organization located in Colorado. OBP was launched in 2010 to develop a response to maritime piracy. The group works to mobilize the maritime community, develop public-private partnerships to promote long-term solutions to piracy, and obtain sustainable deterrence based on the rule of law. OBP also supports the international community in its efforts to bring an end to contemporary maritime piracy. The group's website is a great source of information about piracy. The website's home page contains recent news and an overview of trends in the fight against piracy, and the site includes a library featuring international law documents, reports, and links to other websites. A recent OBP document available online is *The Human Cost of Maritime Piracy 2012.*

Overseas Security Advisory Council (OSAC)
Bureau of Diplomatic Security, US Department of State
Washington, DC   20522-2008

(571) 345-2223 • fax: (571) 345-2238
website: www.osac.gov

The Overseas Security Advisory Council (OSAC), part of the US State Department, was established to promote cooperation between the State Department and private sector businesses on issues of security worldwide. Its creation was the result of the increase in terrorism over the last twenty-five years and the threat against US interests overseas. OSAC produces reports on international maritime piracy and a search of the website under the category of piracy produces a list of government publications on crime and safety matters involving piracy. Examples include: *Piracy in the Gulf of Guinea* and *Somali Piracy Update.*

US Institute of Peace

2301 Constitution Ave. NW, Washington, DC   20037
(202) 457-1700 • fax: (202) 429-6063
website: www.usip.org

The US Institute of Peace is an independent, nonpartisan, national institution established and funded by Congress. Its goals are to help prevent and resolve violent international conflicts; promote post-conflict stability and development; and increase conflict management capacity, tools, and intellectual capital worldwide. A search of the group's website produces various publications on the subject of piracy, including: *Counting the Costs of Somali Piracy* and *Piracy and Peace in the Horn of Africa.*

World Bank

1818 H St. NW, Washington, DC   20433
(202) 473-1000 • fax: (202) 477-6391
website: www.worldbank.org

The World Bank was founded in 1944 as a single institution to facilitate reconstruction following World War II. Today, it is made up of five development institutions devoted to the goal of alleviating worldwide poverty. The five institutions are: the

International Bank for Reconstruction and Development, the International Development Association, the International Finance Corporation, the Multilateral Investment Guarantee Agency, and the International Centre for the Settlement of Investment Disputes. A search of the group's website produces a long list of blogs and other resources on the issue of piracy. Examples include "Piracy's Hidden Tax on Trade" and "Ending Somali Piracy: Go After the System, Not Just the Pirates."

Bibliography

Books

Jay Bahadur   *The Pirates of Somalia: Inside Their Hidden World*. New York: Vintage, 2012.

D.R. Burgess   *The World for Ransom: Piracy Is Terrorism, Terrorism Is Piracy*. New York: Prometheus Books, 2010.

Nigel Cawthorne   *Pirates of the 21st Century: How Modern-Day Buccaneers Are Terrorising the World's Oceans*. London: John Blake Publishing, 2011.

Peter Chalk   *The Maritime Dimension of International Security: Terrorism, Piracy, and Challenges for the United States*. Santa Monica, CA: RAND Publishing, 2008.

Peter H. Eichstaedt   *Pirate State: Inside Somalia's Terrorism at Sea*. Chicago: Lawrence Hill Books, 2010.

Colin Freeman   *Kidnapped: Life as a Hostage on Somalia's Pirate Coast*. London: Monday Books, 2011.

Robin Geiss and Anna Petrig   *Piracy and Armed Robbery at Sea: The Legal Framework for Counter-Piracy Operations in Somalia and the Gulf of Aden*. New York: Oxford University Press, 2011.

Brian J. Hesse   *Somalia: State Collapse, Terrorism and Piracy*. New York: Routledge, 2011.

Michael Hirsh   *Pirate Alley: Commanding Task Force 151 Off Somalia*. Annapolis, MD: Naval Institute Press, 2012.

Angus Konstam   *Piracy: The Complete History*. New York: Osprey Publishing, 2008.

James Kraska   *Contemporary Maritime Piracy: International Law, Strategy, and Diplomacy at Sea*. New York: Praeger, 2011.

Gabriel Kuhn   *Life Under the Jolly Roger: Reflections on Golden Age Piracy*. Oakland, CA: PM Press, 2010.

Martin N. Murphy   *Piracy, Terrorism and Irregular Warfare at Sea: Navies Confront the 21st Century*. New York: Routledge, 2011.

Martin N. Murphy   *Small Boats, Weak States, Dirty Money: Piracy and Maritime Terrorism in the Modern World*. New York: Columbia University Press, 2010.

Martin N. Murphy   *Somalia, the New Barbary? Piracy and Islam in the Horn of Africa*. New York: Columbia University Press, 2011.

Andrew Palmer   *The New Pirates: Modern Global Piracy from Somalia to the South China Sea*. New York: I.B. Tauris, 2013.

John C. Payne   *Piracy Today: Fighting Villainy on the
                       High Seas.* New York: Sheridan
                       House, 2010.

Brooks Tenney   *The Incense Coast: Piracy Around the
                       Horn of Africa.* Mustang, OK:
                       Trafford Publishing, 2010.

Periodicals and Internet Sources

Peter Apps   "Have Hired Guns Finally Scuppered
                       Somali Pirates?" Reuters, February
                       12, 2013. www.reuters.com.

Stephen Askins   "US Presidential Order on Payment
                       of Ransoms and Recent
                       Developments," HG Legal Resources,
                       September 14, 2010. www.hg.org.

Associated Press   "No Somali Pirate Hijacking in
                       Nearly a Year, Says UN," *Guardian*,
                       May 3, 2013. www.theguardian.com.

Michael L. Baker   "Smarter Measures in Fight Against
                       Piracy," Council on Foreign
                       Relations, December 10, 2010.
                       www.cfr.org.

BBC   "West Africa Piracy Overtakes Somali
                       Ship Attacks," June 18, 2013.
                       www.bbc.co.uk.

Max Boot   "Fight Off, Don't Pay Off, Pirates,"
                       Commentary, January 24, 2011.
                       www.commentarymagazine.com.

Douglas R.   "Piracy Is Terrorism," *New York
Burgess Jr.   Times*, December 5, 2008.
                       www.nytimes.com.

Jia Cheng   "Anti-Piracy Training Helping Ship
                       Crews Thwart Attacks," *Global Times*,
                       November 23, 2010. http://military
                       .globaltimes.cn.

CNN   "Despite U.S. Policy, Nothing Stops
                       Ransom Payment, Expert Says," April
                       8, 2009. http://articles.cnn.com.

Alan Cowell   "West African Piracy Exceeds Somali
                       Attacks, Report Says," *New York
                       Times*, June 18, 2013. www.nytimes
                       .com.

The Economist   "What Happened to Somalia's
                       Pirates?" May 19, 2013. www
                       .economist.com.

FoxNews.com   "Somali Pirates Release Sailors as
                       Piracy Reports Reach Five-year Low,"
                       March 12, 2013. www.foxnews.com.

Jeffrey Gettleman   "Suddenly, a Rise in Piracy's Price,"
                       New York Times, February 26, 2011.
                       www.nytimes.com.

Pauline Jelinek   "Admiral: U.S. Should Pursue Pirate
                       Ransoms," *Navy Times*, April 16,
                       2010. www.navytimes.com.

Billy Kenber   "Life Sentences Recommended for
                       Somali Pirates," *Washington Post*,
                       August 2, 2013. http://articles
                       .washingtonpost.com.

Rohit Khanna   "Ship Hijacked by African Pirates,"
                       Times of India, July 17, 2013. http://
                       articles.timesofindia.indiatimes.com.

Mary Kimani "Tackling Piracy off African Shores: More Regional Cooperation Needed for Peace and Security," *Africa Renewal Online*, January 2009. www.un.org.

D.H. Nairobi "Somalia and Piracy: The Cost on Land as Well as at Sea," *The Economist*, April 11, 2013. www.economist.com.

Bambang Hartadi Nugroho "Extending Cooperation to Combat Sea Piracy," *The Jakarta Post*, April 25, 2011. www.thejakartapost.com.

Oceans Beyond Piracy "The Economic Cost of Somali Piracy," 2012. http://oceansbeyondpiracy.org.

Paul Salopek "A Hidden Victim of Somali Pirates: Science," *National Geographic News*, April 25, 2013. http://news/nationalgeographic.com.

Abdi Sheikh and Daniel Fineren "At Least 11 Dead as Ship Held by Pirates Sinks Off Somalia," Reuters, July 8, 2013. http://uk.reuters.com.

Vivienne Walt "Why the Somali Pirates Keep Getting Their Ransoms," *Time*, April 20, 2009. www.time.com.

Lesley Anne Warner "Pieces of Eight: An Appraisal of US Counterpiracy Options in the Horn of Africa," *Naval War College Review*, Spring 2010. www.usnwc.edu.

Sharon
Weinberger

"Intrigue, Brinksmanship Woven Into Hidden World of Pirate Ransoms," *AOL News*, March 27, 2011. www.aolnews.com.

World Bank

"Ending Somali Piracy Will Need On-Shore Solutions and International Support to Rebuild Somalia," April 11, 2013. www .worldbank.org.

World Bank

"The Pirates of Somalia: Ending the Threat, Rebuilding a Nation," 2013. http://siteresources.worldbank.org.

Index

A

Adams, John, 8
AdvanFort Company, 50
Afghanistan, 79
AK-47 weapons, 27
Algerian cargo ship, 49
Allen, Joe, 54–55
Al-Qaeda, 25
Al-Shabaab, 25–27, 30, 59, 71
American Revolution, 8
Andrews, Crispin, 66–75
Anti-pirate programs, 75, 81, 83
Automatic Identification System
    (AIS), 69
Al-Awlaki, Anwar, 30

B

Bahadur, Jay, 83–84
Bahamas, 65
Bahrain, 53
Barbary pirates (corsairs), 8–9, 32
Barre, Mohamed Siad, 25
Bellish, Jon, 33–36
Best Management Practices for
    Protection against Somalia Based
    Piracy (BMP), 16, 41
MV Blida (ship), 49–50
Bird, Bella, 82
Bolton, John R., 29–32, 34–35
British East India Company, 59
Brunei University, 72
Buccaneers, defined, 7

C

Capone, Al, 64
Caribbean pirates, 7
Cassese, Antonio, 35
Chatham House report, 71–72
China, 58
Clinton, Hillary, 38
Coca production, 79
College of International Security
    Affairs, 26
Combined Maritime Forces
    (CMF), 53–54
Comoros, 12
Contact Group on Piracy, 40–41
Corsairs. *See* Barbary pirates
Counter-piracy strategy, 40

D

The Daily Telegraph (newspaper),
    63
Department of International Secu-
    rity Studies, 26
Djibouti, 12
Drake, Francis, 8
Dunne, Philip, 74

E

East Africa, 12–13, 70, 78, 82
Elizabeth I (Queen), 8
Ethiopia, 25
European Union (EU), 47, 50, 58,
    61

F

G

H

I

J

K

L

M